JUDAISM
AND
CHRISTIANITY

The Differences

JUDAISM AND CHRISTIANITY

The Differences

Trude Weiss-Rosmarin, Ph.D.

jD JONATHAN DAVID PUBLISHERS, INC.
Middle Village, New York 11379

JUDAISM AND CHRISTIANITY:
THE DIFFERENCES

by
Trude Weiss-Rosmarin

Copyright © 1997 by Jonathan David Publishers, Inc.

Originally published in 1943 by The Jewish Book Club

Jonathan David Publishers, Inc.
68-22 Eliot Avenue
Middle Village, New York 11379

Library of Congress Cataloging-in-Publication Data

Weiss-Rosmarin, Trude.
  [Judaism & Christianity]
  Judaism & Christianity : the differences / Trude Weiss-Rosmarin.
     p. cm.
  Originally published: Judaism and Christianity. New York : Jewish Book Club,
     c1943.
  ISBN 0-8246-0398-2
  1. Judaism—Relations—Christianity. 2. Christianity and other religions—
judaism. I. Title.
BM535.W43 1997
296.3'96—dc21   97-11944
                                                                    cip
                                                                    r97

This edition designed and composed by John Reinhardt Book Design

Printed in the United States of America

Contents

Introductory Remarks

Is there any need or justification to restate and analyze the differences between Judaism and Christianity in our day? Is not such an endeavor contrary to the "good will" efforts in which Jews and Christians alike see the hope for better understanding and cooperation between the two religions in the world of tomorrow? Is it not detrimental to harmonious Christian-Jewish relations and, especially, to the cause and destiny of Judaism in the Christian world, when the basic differences between the two faiths are emphasized by Jews?

I anticipate such questions and objections to the very theme of this volume. And, I shall confess, it is qualms and scruples of this type that made me hesitate for a long time to approach the task of restating objectively, and with no other regard but for the truth as I see it, the eternal and fundamental differences between Judaism and Christianity. If I finally decided to write this book it was because I arrived at the conclusion that it was high time to stress in *Jewish* circles that "good will" between Jews and Christians should not and must not be synonymous with raising all bars and obliterating or denying the differences that separate the two faiths.

In point of fact, liberal Christians and leaders in "good

will" are far from propounding the idea that there are no dissimilarities between Judaism and Christianity. On the contrary, Christian theologians and Bible scholars, to say nothing of the laity, adhere staunchly to the Christian teachings opposing those of Judaism, and they do not hesitate to state so in clear and unequivocal language. They have no qualms to postulate the differences that set their faith apart from Judaism and to assert, without reluctance, that the Christian doctrines and teachings are superior. Even such a progressive and liberal Bible scholar as Professor Albright does not hesitate to declare that "the trinitarian idea of God has immeasurably enriched the concept of monotheism" (*From the Stone Age to Christianity*, p. 304). And despite the fact that this brilliant scholar applies the tools of critical research to all phases of the Jewish religion, he is beset by qualms to do the same in the case of Christianity. Notwithstanding the fact that his critical mind perceives the obvious pagan and mystical elements in the Gospels and the impossibility of the justification of the Christian messianic claims on scholarly grounds, he does yet not invalidate them, for "the historian cannot settle questions which are outside of his jurisdiction, the decision must be left to the Church and to the individual believer, who are historically warranted in accepting the whole of the messianic framework of the Gospels. . . . The historian, *qua historian*, must stop at the threshold, unable to enter the shrine of the Christian mysteria without removing his shoes, conscious that there are realms where history and nature are inadequate, and where God reigns over them in eternal majesty" (*From the Stone Age to Christianity*, p. 308).

I have brought this quotation from Professor Albright's study on monotheism and the historical progress because it demonstrates to what extent liberal Christian Bible scholars are reluctant to apply the tools of criticism they so freely employ in the dissection and vivisection of Judaism to their own faith and its teachings. Of course, we have no quarrel with them on that score for, obviously, unless one is convinced of the absolute validity of one's religion and its teachings he cannot find salvation in it.

Christians of good will and active on behalf of promoting a better understanding between Jews and Christians, therefore, have never committed the mistake of suggesting that this desirable harmony be achieved at the cost of the sacrifice of their own distinctive beliefs. Liberal and progressive Christians have no scruples to assert that Judaism and Christianity are divided by an unbridgeable chasm, which does not, however, preclude mutual tolerance and good will. Professor Travers Herford, the renowned Bible and Rabbinic scholar, and a genuine admirer of Judaism, did yet state that "Judaism and Christianity can never blend without the surrender by the one or the other of its fundamental principles" (*Jewish Studies in Memory of Israel Abrahams*, 1927, p. 220).

Regrettably, this important point has been dangerously minimized by not a few Jews, zealous advocates of "good will," who, as a result of wishful and unscientific thinking, were deluded into asserting, as did Professor Julian Morgenstern, President of the Hebrew Union College of Cincinnati, in a charge to the students of his College, that "the two religions [Judaism and Christianity] are truly, basically one." Thus, while Professor Morgenstern and numerous rabbis and Jewish leaders and literati sense no contradiction in such terms as "Judeo-Christian" and "Judeo-Christianity," Professor Carl J. Friedrich of Harvard University asks, "What justifies the expression Judeo-Christian culture? Are not Judaism and Christianity fundamentally opposed to each other?" He justifies the expression with the argument that "Christian culture has grown up as much around the Old Testament as around the New" (*Jews in a Gentile World*, edited by I. Graeber and St. H. Britt, Macmillan, 1942, pp. 7f), a circumstance which hardly warrants the use of the expression "Judeo-Christian" by Jews.

We have no objection, however, to Professor Friedrich's definition of "Judeo-Christian" as an acknowledgment of Christianity's debt to Judaism and of the profound influence of the Hebrew Bible on the New Testament. We, and there is ample reason to assume that the vast majority of Christians will second this objection, oppose, however, the use of "Judeo-Christian" in the sense Professor Morgenstern employs it, namely to express that "the two religions are truly, basically one." For, in point of fact, Judaism and Christianity are *not* basically one but are, as Professor Friedrich so aptly states, "fundamentally opposed to each other." Professor Herford was therefore right in prognosticating that "Judaism and Christianity can never blend without the surrender by the one or the other of its fundamental principles." In view of such authoritative Christian statements, it seems strange that Dr. Morgenstern blithely asserts that "we may truthfully call Judeo-Christianity the religion of tomorrow's better world" (*Judaism's Contribution to Post-War Religion*, p. 15).

Dr. Morgenstern's attempts at levelling the differences between Judaism and Christianity, differences that are jealously guarded and defended by even the most liberal Christians, spring from the mistaken notion that "good will" is predicated on identity and the abolition of all existent differences. This, of course, is a fatal misunderstanding. It reminds one of the pathetic efforts of the pioneer suffragettes who believed that in order to win equality with men they had to become men. As a result, these unhappy women simulated masculinity in a most ridiculous way. They sported mannish, unattractive clothes; they spoke in rasping and strident tones; they divested themselves of any and every womanly charm—and all this in order to prove that there is no difference between men and women. If anything it was these affectations that made the cause of the suffragettes so unpopular. Today's women, fortunately, have discovered that holding and filling a man's job and enjoying a man's rights form no contradiction to remaining femininely charming and attractive. On the contrary...

Most Jewish leaders in "good will" efforts are in a state of mind resembling that of the early suffragettes. They, too, believe that they can attain equality in the Christian community only by stressing that there is no difference between Judaism and Christianity. But just as men—and all normal women—will not assent to the preposterous notion that there is no difference between male and female, so all Christians—and all normal Jews uninhibited by inferiority complexes—will insist that Judaism and Christianity are *not* the same. Instead they will point out that "good will" and mutual understanding are not contingent upon regimentation and the levelling of the distinctions and differences between Judaism and Christianity.

The notion that Judaism and Christianity, to maintain harmonious relations, must be "truly, basically one," is really a totalitarian aberration. For democracy is predicated on the conviction that dissimilarities and differences are no cause or justification for inequality. The democratic solution is that those of different views and beliefs should respect the dissimilar views and beliefs of their neighbors. After all, we don't demand that all Americans vote for the same ticket in order to promote national unity. On the contrary, we encourage political differences while expecting that those who differ will do so in a civilized and *constructive* manner.

The example of the "American way" should prove that the differences between Judaism and Christianity, and the emphasis on and analysis of these differences by Jews and Christians, in no way hinder the progress of "good will" and better understanding between Jews and Christians. "Good will" should never mean, for either Jew or Christian, to assimilate his own faith to the religion of those with whom he wants to reach a better understanding and whom he wants to harbor "good will" towards his own religion. Genuine "good will," therefore, is not a levelling of the fundamental Jewish-Christian differences, but, as Professor Herford suggested, the endeavor "to understand and respect each other, and recognize that each religion has God's work to do." If anything, however, such understanding and respect must be predicated on the knowledge and grasp of the differences that distinguish one's own religion from that with whose adherents he wants to live in friendship and harmony.

Unfortunately, there are even in this "enlightened" day and age many prominent Christian theologians who labor under the illusion that the differences between Judaism and Christianity make a real understanding between the two faiths impossible. The stand of this group, large in numbers and prominent in influence, may be gauged from the following excerpt from Dr. Otto Piper's *God in History*, (MacMillan, 1939): "Notwithstanding the many and essential elements which they have in common, there can be no real understanding between them [Judaism and Christianity]. The Church came into existence as a result of the crucifixion of Jesus, and His cross will therefore perpetually separate Jews and Christians. Attempts are made by both Jews and Christians to advocate mutual understanding. If these endeavors are for practical cooperation in social or humanitarian fields, they are legitimate . . . But as soon as they tend to minimize the difference of religious outlook which exists between the two religions, they are bound to fail.

"The Jews may be willing to acknowledge the greatness of Christ, but they only seek thereby to emphasize the greatness of Judaism, for they vindicate Jesus as their greatest son. If they would recognize Him as their Messiah and Savior, they would no longer be able to be Jews . . ." (*op. cit.*, p. 106). Dr. Piper therefore concludes: "There can be no real friendship between Christianity and Judaism, although it can exist between individuals of both groups. For their religions belong to two different aeons" (*op. cit.*, p. 110). Dr. Piper's position as Professor of Systematic Theology at Princeton Theological Seminary and the fact that he occupied the chair of Systematic Theology in the University of Muenster, Germany, as the successor of the famous Protestant theologian, Karl Barth, before leaving Nazi Germany in protest against the regime's persecution of the Protestant Church, should prove that this is an authoritative pronouncement and not merely the opinion of an individual without standing and office.

In delineating the differences between Judaism and Christianity we are doing no more than what Christian theologians have been engaged in since the composition of the Gospels. This statement is not meant as an "apology" but rather as an explanation why we deem it necessary to examine these differences from the Jewish point of view as well.

Our restatement of the differences between Judaism and Christianity, however, is not motivated by the intention to divide the two faiths against each other but impelled by the desire to promote real "good will," the kind that is not built on unstable generalizations. We believe that genuine "good will" can only grow from knowledge, knowledge that is informed by the religious conviction that human beings, in despite that they are different and behave and believe differently, are yet all brothers through their common humanity. This type of "good will" has been advocated by the Jewish prophets, sages and teachers through the ages, even in the long medieval night of cruel persecution at the hands of the Church. It is in this spirit of Jewish "good will" that I shall endeavor to delineate and analyze the differences between Judaism and Christianity.

CHAPTER I

The Jewish and the Christian God Idea

THE CHIEF AND FUNDAMENTAL DIFFERENCE between Judaism and Christianity is that the former is committed to pure and uncompromising monotheism and the latter subscribes to the belief in the trinitarian nature of the Divine Being. Trinitarianism, that is to say, the belief in and worship of "God, the Son and the Holy Spirit" are as basic and important to all types and denominations of Christianity as they are contrary to all and everything Judaism holds sacred. To the unconditional monotheism of Judaism the doctrine of the Trinity is profoundly objectionable, because it is a concession to polytheism or, at any rate, an adulteration of the idea of the One, Unique, Indefinable and *Indivisible* God. The revolutionary feat of early Mosaism was the complete break with the cults of the many deities and the unconditional and unreserved espousal of the Only God. Through the ages the Jewish prophets, sages and teachers have struggled toward a better and more perfect knowledge of the Being of God. Many definitions of God have seen the light in Judaism, which is not bound to any fixed, circumscribed definition beyond the insistence that God is One as a Unity of Oneness that cannot be divided. Different Jewish concepts of God have been evolved in different ages, but there is one point which has always been beyond discussion because of its axiomatic character: the Indivisible Oneness of God, which has always been interpreted as implying qualitative uniqueness no less than quantitative unity.

The "Unity" of God, besides His "Oneness," must be stressed if monotheism is to endure in unadulterated purity. For mere quantitative Oneness permits logically of additions and accretions or divisions, as is evident from Christian Trinitarianism. Once, however, the unique Unity of God is postulated as His chief and most significant characteristic, there is no longer any basis for dividing or adding to the Being of God. Schopenhauer, despite his bitter outbursts against Judaism, yet deserves credit for having recognized this fact in stating that "Judaism cannot be denied the glory of being the only genuine monotheistic religion on earth; there is none beside it that possesses an objective God, the Creator of Heaven and Earth" (*Parerga and Paralipomena I*).

The Jewish tenet of the Unity of God also precludes the belief in any other creative force besides Him. Satan, the power of evil and completely independent of God, plays a very important role in Christianity. Judaism knows of no Satan as a creative force of evil opposed to the benevolent creative power of God. It only knows One Creator, Who made both the light *and* the darkness and Who created in man the good inclination and the evil inclination together with the faculty of free ethical choice. The Jew, therefore, does not fear Satan for, as a pithy Hasidic teaching has it, if one fears anything besides God, one is guilty of idolatry, fear being a kind of tribute to a power of which one is afraid, and tribute should only be offered to God.

Although Judaism wants its followers to meditate and reflect on the Being of God, it also impresses upon them that

God is unknowable and cannot be defined or grasped with the limited intellect of man. But there is one thing we know of God, namely, that He is an Indivisible Unity. This conviction of man's eternal impossibility to really understand and know God, although he may glory in His Oneness, has never been more powerfully expressed than in Solomon Ibn Gabirol's "Royal Crown."

> Thou art One, the first of every number, and the
>   foundation of every structure.
> Thou art One, and at the mystery of Thy Oneness the
>   wise of heart are struck dumb,
> For they know not what it is.
> Thou art One, and Thy Oneness can neither be in-
>   creased nor lessened,
> It lacketh naught, nor doth aught remain over.
> Thou art One, but not like a unit to be grasped or
>   counted,
> For number and change cannot reach Thee.
>
> Thou existest, but hearing of ear cannot reach Thee, or
>   vision of eye.
> Nor shall the How have sway over Thee, nor the
>   Wherefore and Whence.
> Thou existest, but for Thyself and for none other with
>   Thee.
> Thou existest, and before Time began Thou wast,
> And without place Thou didst abide.
> Thou existest, and Thy secret is hidden and who shall
>   attain to it?
> So deep, so deep, who can discover it?*

---

* Translation by Israel Zangwill in: *Selected Religious Poems by Solomon Ibn Gabirol* (1923), pp. 83f.

THE MEDIEVAL PHILOSOPHERS, however, were not the first to enunciate the conviction that man's limited intellect is insufficient for grasping the Being of God. Already Isaiah despaired of the possibility of knowing God through analogy and comparison. "To whom will you liken Me, that I should be equal?" (Isaiah 40:25). He represents the Lord thundering at man whose puny intellect would dare endeavor to unravel the secrets of His Being. God is "unknowable," for to really know Him man would have to possess divine faculties. In the words of Yedaya Ha-Penini, "Could I ever know Him, I would be He."

Judaism, therefore, leaves its followers considerable freedom in the definition of God. This, however, has no bearing on the Being of God as such, for He remains the Absolute Unity of Being despite the different views men may have of Him. Subjective and individualized definitions of God, however, are legitimate only if it is acknowledged that they are, of necessity, but inadequate attempts of bringing the understanding of God nearer to man. "You must not believe," God is represented by the Sages as having addressed Himself to Israel, "that there are many gods in heaven because you have had various visions. Know that I am the Only God" (Shemot Rabba 29:2). The same conviction was sounded by a chasidic rabbi some fifteen centuries later, who explained that the Lord is acclaimed as "God of gods" (Deuteronomy 10:17) to teach us that He is a God defying any definition or conception of His being; that is to say, "He is exalted above any conception of Him of which man is capable."

The view that God cannot be defined by any positive, definitive attributes was carried to victory by the staunch rationalist Maimonides. The motive of his reluctance of describing God in terms of human attributes was the recognition that man cannot know what God is although he is capable of knowing what God is *not* and cannot be, namely, anything resembling a creature of blood and flesh, or any form of inorganic matter or organic structure. Instead of describing God by means of positive attributes, He was therefore defined with negative attributes. So that, instead of saying that God is active, the medieval rationalist Jewish philosophers stated that He is not *in*active, etc.

THERE IS AN UNBROKEN CONTINUITY in Jewish tradition and creativeness. This does not mean that nothing new was added to Jewish culture through the ages, but only that all new accretions and creations were of one spirit, as it were, with all that preceded and succeeded them. As a result we find the tendency of professing *what God is not*, rather than *what He is*, already active in biblical times. In impressing upon Israel the incorporeal character of the Divine Revelation at Sinai, Deuteronomy insists: "Ye heard the voice of words, but ye saw *no* form; only a voice" (Deuteronomy 4:12). Consequently, there follows the warning: "Take ye therefore good heed unto yourselves—for ye saw no manner of form on the day that the Lord spoke unto you in Horeb out of the midst of fire" (Deuteronomy 4:15).

If Maimonides laid down in his Code that "whosoever conceives God to be a corporeal being is an apostate" (Hilchot Teshuvah 3:7), he only drew the logical conclusion from the sum total of biblical teachings and talmudic reasoning.

Nothing probably is so foreign to Judaism as regimentation. To be sure, there has always been discipline, but within the clearly defined space of the Law there was a most remarkable latitude of freedom of expression. Thanks to this respect for the "minority opinion" we find in the Bible, and especially in talmudic literature, also statements that describe God in almost shockingly corporeal terms. Side by side, almost, with such statements as: "We describe Him by figures borrowed from His creatures so that the ear may get it . . ." (Mechilta to Exodus 19:18), and that in the world-to-come the Unity of God will be such that He will be known by but one name (Pesachim 50a), we find numerous statements which can only be understood correctly if we regard them as symbolisms or "anthropomorphic concessions" to those who found it impossible to find spiritual solace in the worship of an invisible and indefinable God. There were, besides the philosophically minded Sages, who thought of God in spiritual terms exclusively, also teachers who were inclined to believe that God was the physical "model" of man created in His image, only that He commanded perfection in all His ways. These more mystically inclined Rabbis interpreted God's goodness to mean that He blesses the grooms, adorns the brides, visits the sick, buries the dead and consoles the mourners (Bereshit Rabba 8:13). He is represented as complying with the commandments of the phylacteries and the wearing of the prayer shawl (Rosh Hashanah 17b). He is said to study the Torah three hours a day (Avoda Zara 3b) and to occupy Himself with most deeds and actions recommended as meritorious to man.

In comparison, however, with the imposing bulk of statements and teachings concerning the pure spirituality and absolute incorporeality of God, these imaginative opinions of naive souls hardly count. They are recorded, however, because the Jewish literary conscience has always adhered to tolerance. The authoritative Jewish belief in God is Maimonides' belief, summed up in his "Thirteen Articles of Faith" as follows: "I believe with perfect faith that the Creator, blessed be His Name, has no bodily form, and that no form can represent Him." Part of the Jew's daily prayer, this confession of faith is his guiding star in the quest for God. Whatever God may be, He is not a body, and must not be represented in any bodily form. This conviction accounts for the "pictureless barrenness" of the Jewish houses of worship, from which any and every "form" is banned as a potential distraction from the concentration on the incomparably unique spirituality of God.

The Unity of God, sacred to Judaism beyond all else, is utterly irreconcilable with the Christian idea of the divisibility of the Divine Being and, above all, with the belief in incarnation. According to Jewish belief God is pure spirit, eternally transcendent and divorced from even the slightest vestige of corporeality. Christianity, on the other hand, asserts that God became man in Jesus, a teaching which is contrary to the very spirit of Judaism. It would be mistaken to assume that modern Protestantism in any way disavows the belief that God became man in Jesus. Even such a progressive Protestant theologian as Dr. John A. Mackay unflinchingly asserts that "the Christian faith is that God was in Christ" (*Christian Message for the World Today*, 1934, p. 116). And the Message of the 1937 Oxford Conference laid down that "The very basis of our faith is self-revelation of God in Jesus Christ . . . for us men and for our salvation he was made man." In other words, as Dr. Harry Emerson Fosdick puts it, "Christianity is the religion of incarnation, and its central affirmation is that God can come into human life" (*The Modern Use of the Bible*, 1924, p. 263).

Is not this contrary to all Jewish teachings of God which emphasize and stress that God is *not* like man and can never become man or even resemble man? Judaism has always fought, and with all weapons at its disposal, against the Christian idea of incarnation, that is to say, of God's coming into human life. The thought that "God was made man" is shocking beyond words to the Jew who believes that God is One and Unique, and that this Uniqueness consists also in His utter difference from anything and everything in existence and anything and everything man can possibly fashion in his mind and label "God." How, then, can the Jewish and Christian ideas of God be reconciled, or how can it be said that the "two religions are truly, basically one"? Is the One and Unique God, the absolute Unity—unknowable, indefinable—really the same as the Christian Trinity which *divides* the Unity of God into three, namely, God the Father, Jesus the Son and the Holy Spirit? Is the Jewish transcendent and purely spiritual belief in a God in Whom there is no trace of matter and Who can never become corporeal really the same as Christian belief which glories in God who "was made man"?

Despite the Jewish insistence on the incorporeality and pure spirituality of God, He has yet been a reality, living and vital, to Jews throughout the ages. God has invariably been a *personal God* to the worshipful Jew, although He was never degraded into *person*. It is important to realize the true meaning of a *personal God* Who is in no respect identical with a *personified God*. Belief in a *personal God* is predicated on the conviction that the Lord of the Universe, though unimaginably superior to and exalted above man is yet near and accessible to him. This belief, however, is not dependent upon the assumption that God is a *person* or possessed of the traits and characteristics generally associated with man. It merely implies, as the Rabbis put it, that although "He is exalted above His world, still when a man enters the House of Prayer, stands behind a pillar and prays in a whisper, the Holy One, blessed be He, will hear his prayer. . . for God is as near to his creatures as the mouth to the ear" (Yerushalmi, Berachot 13a). Such a view quite naturally inspired the comforting conclusion of the Sages that God, when proclaiming the Ten Commandments, introduced Himself as "*thy* God," employing the singular form, in order to teach that "He is the God of every man, woman and child" (Yalkut Shimoni #286).

This awareness and certainty of the nearness of God to all those who seek Him, notwithstanding His unfathomable remoteness from any attribute or faculty that can be grasped with the human intellect, made it unnecessary for Judaism to "humanize" God for the sake of bringing Him nearer to the soul and its *human* needs. Judaism, therefore, has no need for the kind of religious assurances and consolations that Christianity finds in the doctrine of the incarnation of God in Jesus. On the contrary, this doctrine seems to the Jew an infringement upon and a diminution of the incomparable Uniqueness and Unity of God.

In an authoritative study of Christianity we find this definition: "Christianity is a personal-ethical monotheism: the Ultimate is spirit, is person, is one, and is good" (Harris F. Rall, *Christianity*, p. 83).

Such a concept of God is diametrically opposed to that to which Judaism adheres. For Judaism is an ethical monotheism *not* predicated on a person: the Ultimate is spirit, *but not a person*; He is one, but the mystery of this Oneness is unfathomable, although, of this Jews have always felt certain, it is indivisible into three-thirds, all part of the One, as Christianity teaches.

JEWISH MONOTHEISM is not only the negation of the many gods but also the rejection of the personification of God on the one hand and of the deification of human beings on the other. Judaism's refusal to worship Jesus is therefore not only due to its repudiation of the doctrine of incarnation, the belief that God became a person, but equally so to its defiant resistance to all and any attempts of according Divine qualities and honors to mere mortals.

It has been pointed out that the gulf separating Judaism from Catholicism is wider and deeper than the chasm which parts Judaism and Protestantism, for the latter abolished many Hellenistic concepts and practices which the early Church adopted. It is important, however, to understand that the differences between Judaism and Protestantism are less pronounced only in *quantity* but not in *quality*. We shall perceive this readily upon examining the attitudes of Catholicism and Protestantism to the worship of persons.

Catholicism as well as Protestantism worships persons and the images of persons. However, while Catholicism venerates in addition to Jesus a large and still expanding pantheon of Saints and their relics, besides devoting a special cult to the worship of the "Mother of God," Protestantism adores only Jesus in addition to "the Father." Judaism, however, summarily rejects the worship of persons, regardless of whether it be one or many, and so it is no less irreconcilable with Protestantism than with Catholicism. It is therefore idle to speculate on whether Judaism is closer to Protestantism than to Catholicism, for in point of fact, it is so far removed from either that the somewhat lesser distance separating it from Protestantism is of no significance. We shall appreciate this the better upon examining at closer range the traditional Jewish attitude to the deification of mortals.

Before doing so, however, we shall have to pause for a moment to probe the differences between the Jewish and the Christian attitudes to image worship. *Judaism*, through the ages, has been uncompromisingly faithful to the very letter of the second commandment prohibiting the *making* of images and not merely their worship, although *individual Jews* occasionally transgressed this law. Christianity has been less severe in the application of the second commandment. Catholicism especially has made considerable concessions to heathen concepts, concessions that Protestantism was not ready to grant. The fact, however, that Catholics pray not only before the crucifix but also before the images of the "Mother of God" and of the Saints, while Protestantism has banned all pictures and statues with the exception of the crucifix does not bring Protestantism any nearer in *quality* to Judaism, which shrinks from the very thought of offering up prayers before any object, regardless of its symbolic significance. As a result of the aversion to any material symbol of veneration, the early Tannaites already interpreted allegorically the incident of "the fiery serpent" recorded in the Pentateuch. It will be remembered that when the children of Israel were harassed by poisonous snakes, as punishment for their lack of faith, God instructed Moses: "Make thee a fiery serpent, and set it upon a pole; and it shall come to pass, that every one that is bitten, when he seeth it, shall live" (Numbers 21:8). Ostensibly, this was a dangerously close approach to image worship. The Rabbis, therefore, hastened to point out that this story is an allegory, "for can a serpent slay, or keep alive? It is merely to show that when Israel looked toward heaven and kept their hearts in submission to their Father in heaven, they were healed; otherwise they wasted away" (Rosh Hashanah 29a).

The Rabbis' interpretation of the story of the fiery serpent proves to what extent the aversion to image worship is ingrained in Judaism. Of course, the Jew is well aware of the fact that intelligent Christians do not pray to and worship the crucifix but the one whom it represents. Nevertheless, he cannot regard the place of the crucifix in the Christian ritual otherwise than as an offense against the second commandment which prohibits not only the worship of images but their very fabrication, which so easily leads to the graver sin.

JUDAISM HAS BEEN SINGULARLY JEALOUS in guarding the Uniqueness of God. It has therefore consistently refused to either assent to representing that Uniqueness in any material form or to grant to any man the possibility of sharing in that Uniqueness. It is for this reason that Judaism has been zealously insisting upon keeping the domain of God and the realm of man apart. This is why from its very inception it has denied the possibility of any man's, even the most perfect, attaining Divine perfection. To Judaism man is man and God is God and shall remain God in unequalled and eternal majesty. It is instructive to trace how zealously all Jewish sources, from the Bible to the rationalist philosophers, stress the point that no mortal ever attained Divine perfection. Thus Moses, the lawgiver and "master of the prophets," was represented as nothing else but a man, more pious, of course, possessed of a keener mind, certainly, than most mortals—but still only a man. Moses also sinned and he was punished for his transgression. Moses also loved life and was afraid of death, for he was a man and not a divine being. Judaism, alert to the danger of deification lurking in the shadow of a personality as towering as Moses, emphasized consistently his human character. "The man Moses" he is referred to in the Pentateuch. And because Judaism wanted to keep him "the man Moses" it even concealed his grave, lest later generations come to worship there and pray to Moses . . . .

Maimonides postulated the faith in the truth of Moses' prophecy (Moses' *prophecy*, but not Moses, the man) as one of the cardinal Jewish beliefs, summing up the Jewish consensus on Moses as follows: "He was the master of all the prophets who preceded him, and those who followed him were all his inferiors" (Commentary on the Mishnah, Introduction to Chelek). Yet, when this most perfect of all prophets and teachers implored God: "Show me, I pray Thee, Thy Glory" (Exodus 33:18), God explained to him, to quote Maimonides, "that this was impossible since his intellect was bound to matter, that is to say, he was a human being. He [God] therefore said to him: 'For man shall not see me and live'" (Exodus 33:20; Maimonides' "Eight Chapters" VII). In other words, when Moses presumed to invade the eternal enigma of the Divine, he was rejected and assigned to his own sphere, the sphere of all mortals.

Moses has remained in Judaism what he was from the very beginning: a human being. Jews do not believe *in Moses*, but, as Maimonides put it, *in Moses' prophecy*, that is to say, in his message. Maimonides is very explicit in stressing, in another context, that the Divine character of the revelation of the Torah in no way conferred divinity upon Moses. For "in handing down the Torah, Moses was like a scribe writing from dictation the whole of it . . . It is in this sense that he is called 'lawgiver'" (Introduction to Chelek).

The results of this cursory inquiry into the estimate of Moses' character and role should make it clear why Judaism has consistently refused to recognize Jesus and the divine perfection ascribed to him. Judaism has never conceded divine honors to any man born of woman. "The *man* Moses" has been its watchword through the ages; thus it has warded off all attempts to enthrone any mortal as God. With equal consistency it has refused to admit the possibility of any man's sharing in God's perfection, or the incarnation of God in any human being.

Persons, therefore, are not glorified in the Jewish religion. Not one of the Jewish festivals is centered in persons, no matter how great a part certain individuals may have had in the events commemorated. Although Moses was the leader of Israel's liberation from Egypt and of the exodus, he is not glorified in the *Haggadah*, the prayer service for the *Seder* celebrations commemorating the exodus. Obviously, this omission is not accidental but motivated by the consistent tendency to steer clear of glorifying the merits and the impor-tance of great men, a tribute which may easily lead to hero worship and the deification of persons.

While Judaism has rigorously excluded any vestige of hero worship from its festival rituals, the Christian holidays are all, without exception, centered in persons; in Protestantism in Jesus, and in Catholicism, besides in Jesus, also in the "Mother of God" and in the many Saints. This difference implies considerably more than the emphasis on persons in the one religion and the absence of that emphasis in the other. It really amounts to it that Judaism retains in all respects and unconditionally the unadulterated purity of absolute monotheism which has been relinquished to a considerable extent in all forms of Christianity.

CHAPTER II

Miracles

Miracles play a minor role in Judaism. In point of fact, as it has been emphasized especially by Sa'adya Gaon, Maimonides and other authoritative thinkers and teachers, the Jewish belief in the truth of the Divine revelation on Sinai and the trust in Moses as the most perfect prophet and teacher are not at all predicated or dependent upon the miraculous events connected with the Giving of the Law and on the wonders performed by Moses.

Already in early rabbinic literature we find the opinion that biblical miracles were not supernatural occurrences, that is to say, contrary to the laws of nature, but incidents that were perfectly within its Divinely appointed scope. To the Sages of the Talmud as, some fifteen centuries later, to Spinoza and the Deist philosophers, divine interference with the laws of nature seemed illogical and irreconcilable with the grandeur and greatness of God. They therefore boldly declared that God provided for the miracles at the creation, thus answering the objection that it is unthinkable that God would change the laws of nature having appointed them. In accordance with this tendency to take the miraculous out of miracles, Rabbi

Johanan taught: "God made a contract with the Red Sea that it should be divided for the Israelites." His colleague, Rabbi Jeremiah the son of Eleazar, went a step further and remarked that God made a similar contract, among others, with the sun and the moon to halt in their paths at Joshua's command; with the ravens to feed Elijah; with the fire not to harm Hananiah, Mishael and Azariah; with the lions not to hurt Daniel; with the heavens to open up for Ezekiel; and with the fish to spit out Jonah (Bereshit Rabba V, 5).

In keeping with this rationalizing tendency among the best minds of the Sages, we find in the Talmud an enumeration of miraculous things that were created in the twilight of the Sabbath eve of the first world week and then preserved by God to be revealed at the appointed time in the future. Among the supernatural things that were *created*, and consequently not brought into being by interference with the laws of nature, were "the mouth of the earth" which opened up to swallow Korach and his followers; "the mouth of the well" which provided water for the Israelites in the desert; the mouth of Balaam's remarkable talking ass; the rainbow, the manna, Moses' rod, and some more things which the Sages regarded as miraculous (Pesachim 54a; compare "Sayings of the Fathers" V, 9).

Another method of explaining the biblical miracles, which was perfected by the medieval philosophers, was to allegorize them. Sa'adya Gaon, who carried this system to victory, was, however, not the first to employ it. The Midrash already records allegorical interpretations of biblical miracles that attest the rational trend of mind of the earlier Sages. Thus, for instance, Rabbi Nehemiah wanted to explain the miracle at the Red Sea as a reward for Israel's trust in God. He deduced this from the passage: "And the people believed . . ." (Exodus 4:31). His colleague, Rabbi Isaac, however, being dissatisfied with such a rationalization, objected: "They saw all the miracles which were performed for them. How, then, could they not believe?" But matters were not left at that, for another Sage, Rabbi Simeon the son of Abba, supported Rabbi Nehemiah's allegorizing attempt with the statement: "Still, it was because of Abraham's trust in the Holy One, blessed be He, that they were privileged to sing the song at the Red Sea" (Shemot Rabba XXIII, 5).

Even more striking is the allegorical exposition of the Biblical passage: "And it came to pass, when Moses held up his hand that Israel prevailed, and when he let down his hand, Amalek prevailed" (Exodus 17:11). The Rabbis skeptically remarked: "Could, then, the hands of Moses make the battle or break the battle?" And they decided that this action of Moses had only a symbolical significance. "For as long as the Israelites looked upward and kept their hearts in submission to their Father in heaven they prevailed; otherwise, they were defeated" (Rosh Hashanah 29a). This remarkable interpretation is followed by the no less remarkable explanation of the "fiery serpent" as a symbol of directing one's thoughts on high which we have already quoted (see Chapter I, p. 26).

This type of allegorical Bible interpretation was perfected by Sa'adya Gaon and carried to its ultimate limit by Maimonides and his school. Sa'adya even went to the extent of declaring the allegorical interpretation of Biblical passages in conflict with reason or experience a religious duty, for it is a pious act to bring the religious sources into harmony with the accepted truth.

In accordance with the same rationalizing tendency Maimonides went on record that all the miraculous events associated with the careers of the prophets were part of their prophetic visions but did not happen in reality (*Guide of the Perplexed*, Part III, Chapter 46). By characterizing as "prophetic visions" virtually all miraculous events recorded in the Bible, Maimonides contrived to save the rational integrity of Judaism. In this manner he interpreted Abraham's and Jacob's encounters with angels, Joshua's vision of an angel, and similar narratives not as records of actual events but as "prophetic visions" (*Guide of the Perplexed,* Part II, Chapters 41–42). The result of this type of exegesis was that the value of the Bible was no longer sought in those narratives involving belief in miracles but in its ethical teachings and "correct opinions."

IT WOULD BE MISTAKEN, of course, to assume that there was no opposition to the rationalists who reinterpreted the miracles as allegories and prophetic visions. There were always believers who held that the literal acceptance of the Bible is preferable and more soul-satisfying than its rationalization. Nevertheless, there is abundant evidence that the best Jewish minds and the leading teachers have always been arrayed in support of the rational interpretation of Judaism and its sources. Still, the dissenters, who placed the heart above the head and intuition above reasonable cognition, were also accorded the opportunity of justifying and explaining their position. As a result, the Talmud and rabbinic literature present side by side the views of the naive believers and those of the rationalizing intellectuals. Nevertheless, although the Talmud, the faithful and virtually complete record of Jewish life in its totality during roughly a thousand years, registers the popular superstitions and superstitious practices and beliefs current among the plain people and also among some of the Rabbis, it also shows that the best minds among the Sages consistently endeavored to minimize the role of miracles as props of belief.

This difference of opinion as regards the religious value of miracles is strikingly illumined by a discussion between a rather obscure Rabbi Joseph and the eminent Abaye on the following "miracle": It once happened that a woman died and left her poverty-stricken husband with an infant to care for.

He could not afford to hire a wet nurse. And then a miracle happened: his breasts opened up like the breasts of a woman so that he could nurse the child. On this story Rabbi Joseph commented: "Behold, how great this man was that such a miracle was performed for him!" But Abaye objected: "On the contrary, how bad this man was that the world's order was changed on his account" (Shabbat 53b). We see from this that Abaye, who lived almost sixteen hundred years ago, was thoroughly modern, at least as modern as Spinoza and Leibnitz, in disparaging the supernatural interference with the appointed laws of nature as something perverse, rather than glorifying it as a miracle. As a result of such an attitude, the "miracle-worker" was regarded with distrust and even sort of an angry suspicion by the Rabbis. That this was the attitude, at least, of the leading Sages is attested by the fact that Rabbi Simeon Ben Shetah adjudged Honi, the mystical "circle-drawer," as deserving of excommunication when he produced much needed rain by means of magical prayers (Taanit 23a).

The foremost Sages maintained that miracles cannot be invoked in support of the truth, or to prove the correctness of an interpretation or opinion. There is a remarkable story in the Talmud which tells how Rabbi Eliezer, once being unable to convince his colleagues of the correctness of his opinion, performed a number of miracles without the slightest success in swaying them to his side. For when a carob tree was moved a hundred yards from its place as a miraculous testimony in support of Rabbi Eliezer's opinion, the Rabbis shrugged it off, "One does not adduce proof from a carob tree!" Rabbi Eliezer then caused the water to flow backwards, and the walls of the House of Study to incline—and even a heavenly voice proclaimed that he was right. But the Sages would have none of it. And so Rabbi Jeremiah boldly declared, with a pun on the Pentateuchal passage "*it* [*the Torah*] *is not in heaven . . .*" (Deuteronomy 30:12): "The Torah was given to us on Sinai, and so we pay no heed to a heavenly voice" (Bava Metzia 59b). In other words, miracles are rejected as proof of the truth and, more especially, as attestations of the correctness of a certain interpretation of the Torah.

In point of fact, the distrust of the value of the miracle is already clearly expressed in the Pentateuch. Deuteronomy warns against "a prophet, or a dreamer of dreams" who will perform signs and miracles and then, on their strength, ask the people to serve strange gods (Deuteronomy 13:2ff). "Thou shalt not hearken unto the words of that prophet!" is the Biblical exhortation, for the miracles he performs are, according to the Pentateuch, merely an instrument by means of which "Your God putteth you to proof, to know whether ye do love the Lord your God with all your heart and with all your soul." But they cannot serve as proof of the truth of something that is untrue. In the same spirit Maimonides declared that a miracle cannot prove the impossible, that is to say something inherently untrue, for it is "useful solely as a confirmation of that which is possible." (*Guide of the Perplexed*, Part III, 24).

Once, however, miracles are denied the power of proof and are regarded merely as a secondary confirmation of the established truth, they lose virtually all importance. And this is precisely what happened in Judaism. From the first timid biblical disavowal of the value of proof adduced from miracles to the bolder statements of the Sages and, finally, to the rejection of the supernatural by the medieval philosophers, Judaism has progressively disparaged miracles as props of faith. Accordingly, both Sa'adya Gaon and Maimonides could declare that Jewish belief is not predicated on miracles. In keeping with this conviction, Maimonides pictured the Messianic age in utterly this-worldly and realistic hues, warning the believers: "Let it not enter your mind that the Messiah must necessarily perform signs and miracles, do something unprec-

edented, or revive the dead, or do something similar . . ."
(*Mishneh Torah*, Hilchot Melachim XI, 3). Not the performance of miracles is the credential of the Messiah but his
fulfillment of the prophetic promises of a better world of justice and righteousness. In other words, the miracle has no
special religious significance for the Jew, because, as Moses
Mendelssohn on good precedence and authority wrote to a
Christian corespondent, miracles can be used to prove the
truth of any religion and, consequently, cannot be accepted
as proof of any.

IN CONTRADISTINCTION to Judaism's reserved attitude toward
miracles and their rejection as affirmations of religious truths
is their evaluation by Christianity. Miracles play an inordi-
nately important role in Christianity. The Gospels are one
long record of the miracles performed by Jesus. It is significant that, while Judaism refuses to acknowledge miracles as
proof of Divine authorization, the Gospels adduce Jesus'
miraculous acts, such as his revival of the dead, the healing of
the incurables, the transformation of water into wine, and
similar miracles as cogent proofs not only of his Divine authorization but of his Divinity, as it were. Even more significant, however, is the fact that Judaism has no dogmas involving the belief in miraculous events in the terrestrial sphere.
Christianity, on the other hand, is predicated on numerous
doctrines of this kind, such as the incarnation, the Divine
character and perfection of Jesus and the Virgin Birth.

Whereas Judaism emphasizes the importance of reasonable cognition for the establishment of religious truth and
refuses to accord to the miraculous any value whatsoever in
ascertaining or affirming the truth, Christianity postulates the
superiority of belief in miracles—unquestioning, blind belief
as against reasonable cognition. Tertullian, one of the early

Church Fathers, expressed this Christian attitude in the classical dictum, *credo quia absurdum est*—"I believe because it is absurd," a manner of argumentation which is utterly foreign to the Jewish mind and irreconcilable with Jewish principles stressing knowledge and reason as indispensable props of faith.

As a result of this overemphasis of the supernatural, Christianity, especially in its Catholic form, has virtually become a slave to miracles. Catholicism chooses its Saints on the strength of the miracles they performed or because of the wonders that were made manifest through them. Thus, while Judaism maintains that the miracles are unimportant, secondary demonstrations of which the religious leader may make use, for the sake of expediency, Catholicism asserts that the experience or performance of miracles is the acid test of the truth of the religious mission of the Saint and the *sine qua non* of canonization. Moreover, the Church's approval of such miracle cults as that of the Virgin of Lourdes, for example, even today, shows that Catholicism still adheres to Tertullian's principle of *credo quia absurdum est.*

As the result of the large part miracles played in the birth and early history of Christianity, Christian worship, Catholic as well as Protestant, revolves around the mysteries of the sacraments, numbering seven in the Catholic Church and two in the Protestant confessions. Baptism and the Lord's Supper, the two sacraments recognized by all Christian denominations, are thoroughly imbued with mystical and miraculous elements. Thus baptism is believed to cleanse the newborn from "original sin" and to save him from eternal perdition. The Lord's Supper and the partaking of the Eucharist and the sacramental wine is regarded as the establishment of a direct, physical bond between the believers and Jesus, of whose body and blood they symbolically partake by eating the Eucharist and drinking the wine of Communion.

Judaism, which freed itself from the last vestiges of mythological concepts in worship with the abolition of the sacrifices about two thousand years ago, has no sacraments. Its very spirit is irreconcilable with the mythological concept of Transubstantiation (the belief in the transformation of the wafer into the body of Christ and of the wine into his blood) sacred to all confessing Christians. Judaism makes salvation solely dependent upon the free will ethical efforts of the worshipper. The ritual of the synagogue, therefore, knows of no prayer, sacrament or symbolism through which salvation can be magically attained.

It would be futile to argue that "modern" Christians do not subscribe to these beliefs and that this dissimilarity between Judaism and Christianity is therefore no longer apparent. In point of fact, Catholicism has not at all changed its attitude to miracles and the sacraments. That the Protestant reformation was a social revolt of the laity against the tutelage and domination of the clergy rather than a revolt against the miracles is evident from the fact that Luther himself firmly believed in apparitions of the devil and similar miraculous visions. Besides, Protestantism in retaining the sacraments of baptism and the Lord's Supper has also retained their mystical interpretation, although it democratized their dispensation. Except for a few radical reformers, whose influence in the Church may be compared to that of a few drastic reformers in the Synagogue, Protestants accept the miracles recorded in the New Testament at face value and abide by the basic teachings of Christianity with which miracles are inseparably interwoven. Christian belief in its various Protestant interpretations is therefore still "justified by faith" in contradistinction to Judaism which makes "the knowledge of God" the first prerequisite of belief.

Thanks to the efforts of generations upon generations of rabbis and thinkers, who applied the light of reason to every tenet and teaching of Judaism, there is virtually nothing in *authoritative* Jewish belief (of course, there are popular superstitions) that is contrary to reason and the laws of nature. To give but one illustration: the belief in Elijah's ascent to heaven in a fiery chariot is unimportant from the viewpoint of Judaism and may consequently be explained allegorically. Jesus' ascension, however, is very important to Christianity and to interpret it allegorically would amount to depriving the Christian religions of their very basis and justification. Paul, therefore, was right in warning the Corinthians against any doubt in Jesus' resurrection, for "if Christ was not raised, there is nothing in our message; there is nothing in our faith either, and we are found guilty of misrepresenting God, for we have testified that He raised Christ" (I Corinthians 15:14f).

Thanks to its complete freedom from the compulsion of the belief in miracles Judaism has stood up better than Christianity in the face of the emergence of modern science. The theory of evolution is not necessarily contrary to the spirit of Judaism and its interpretation of creation, for there is an early rabbinic statement to the effect that the creation of the world, as we know it, was preceded by the creation and destruction of other worlds (Bereshit Rabba III, 7).

The Jewish belief in God as the Incomparable and only Unified Creative Power is not affected by whether we assume that creation was one single act or a continuous process, for does not the Jew daily render thanks unto God "who reneweth the work of creation every day?" As a result, the zeal the Church displayed in suppressing the "heresies" of such men as Copernicus, Giordano Bruno and numerous other scientists who paid a high price for their scholarly integrity and daring would be impossible in Judaism which has always endeavored to *understand* the Creator and Creation rather than accept Him and His wondrous works on faith alone, especially if such faith involves the unqualified belief in miracles.

CHAPTER III

Free Will
vs. Original Sin

JEWISH ETHICS is predicated on the trust in man's ethical freedom, the faculty of choice between good and evil. The medieval Jewish philosophers therefore postulated, on the strength of biblical and rabbinic pronouncements, that there would be no room for commandments and prohibitions and for reward and punishment if man were not free to choose his conduct.

The authoritative Jewish sources emphasize that all human beings are endowed with freedom in the ethical sphere and are not constrained to pursue a certain path. "I have set before thee life and death, the blessing and the curse; therefore choose life, that thou mayest live . . ." (Deuteronomy 30:15) is the perennial watchword of Jewish ethics. The characteristic Jewish avowal of complete ethical freedom is perhaps most strikingly set forth in the "Wisdom of Sirach":

> Do not say, "It was because of the Lord that I fell away."
> For He will not do things that He hates.
> Do not say, "It was He that led me astray."
> For He has no need of a sinner.

The Lord hates anything abominable;
And left him in the hands of his own decision;
If you will, you can keep the commandments,
And acting faithfully rests on your own pleasure.
He has set fire and water before you;
Stretch out your hand for whichever you wish.
Life and death are before a man,
And whichever he chooses will be given him.
(Sirach 15:11–20)

The conviction that man is "in the hands of his decision" was especially insistently sounded by the talmudic Sages, who taught that "everything is in the hands of God—except the fear of God" (Berachot 33b). In other words, God determines and guides man's fortunes but He does not influence or interfere with his ethical conduct. This view is also stressed in the Agadic representation of what transpires on-high in the hour of the child's conception: The angel Lailah places the seminal drop from which the new human being is to grow before God and asks: "Lord of the Universe, what is to become of this drop? Is it to develop into a strong or a weak person, into one who is wise or foolish, rich or poor? *But nothing is said whether he will be wicked or righteous*" (Niddah 16b). Ostensibly, God guides only man's destiny but does not determine his conduct, besides enabling him to choose between good and evil. The Sages accordingly held that the eye, the ear and the nostrils cannot be controlled, but the organs regulated by the voluntary muscles, such as the mouth, the hands and the feet are in man's power (Midrash Tanhuma, ed. Buber, Toldot 21). We hear, whether we want it or not, whatever sounds are received by the ears. But the reaction to what we hear is determined by our free will decision, for all the organs through which man translates his ethical or unethical intentions into actions are controlled by voluntary muscles. Yehudah Halevi therefore correctly stated that "man has the power to sin or to abstain from sin in regard to those things that are committed to his control" (*Kuzari* V, 20).

The conviction that God controls only the fortune and destiny of man but leaves him complete freedom in the ethical sphere, moved the Sages to lay down the principle that "all things are foreseen, yet free will is granted" (Sayings of the Fathers III, 15). And so "he who wants to defile himself will find all the gates open. And he who desires to purify himself will be able to do so" (Shabbat 104a), for "man is led along the road which he wants to follow" (Makkot 10b).

Free decision is the very foundation of ethics, for without the temptation and the *possibility* (but not constraint!) to sin piety would not be meritorious. A pithy rabbinic lesson, therefore, stresses that we should not become oblivious to our ability to act contrary to the commandments. "One should not say: 'I cannot eat pork; I cannot enter into a forbidden sexual relation.' Instead one should say, 'I could act thus, but how may I do so against the command of my Father in Heaven'" (Sifra to Leviticus 20:26). The "saint" free from the tug of temptation is definitely not the prototype of Jewish piety. On the other hand, however, Judaism has steered clear of making man helplessly subject to the compulsion of sin. The avowed belief of Judaism is that "the Creator does not influence the actions of man" (Sa'adya, Emunot VeDeoth VI, 10). All depends on his free choice. To quote Nahmanides, "he can act or not act" (Commentary to Genesis 22:1).

Maimonides, the great master of the art of summation, has also admirably epitomized the accepted Jewish attitude on free will: "Man is endowed with free will," he declares categorically. "It is therefore reasonable that the Torah contains commandments and prohibitions with announcements of reward and punishment." Furthermore, "the doctrine of man's absolute free will is one of the cardinal principles of the

Torah of our teacher Moses, and of those who follow the Torah. According to this principle, man does what is in his power to do, by his nature, his choice and his will" (*Guide of the Perplexed* III, 17). Once, however, it is accepted that man is endowed with free will, it follows that he is responsible for his righteous or unrighteous conduct. Maimonides summarizes the traditional Jewish viewpoint as follows: "Free will is granted to every man. If he wants to accustom himself to righteousness and become righteous, he is free to do so; and if he wants to follow evil and become wicked, he is free to do so, as it is written in the Torah, 'Behold, the man is become as one of us, to know good and evil'. . . . Every man can become as righteous as Moses our teacher or as wicked as Jeroboam; he can be wise or stupid, kind or cruel, miserly or liberal, and so it is with all the other qualities. There is no compelling, forcing or pulling him in either direction, but he himself, of his own accord and mind, follows the path he prefers . . . . And this is a cardinal principle of our faith, a pillar of the Torah and the commandments. . . . For were God to decree that a man be righteous or wicked, or if there were anything in his basic constitution forcing him in either of the two ways . . . how could He have commanded us through the Prophets, act thus and not thus, mend your ways and do not go after your wickedness, if from his very creation his conduct had been decreed for him, or if his constitution would force him to something he cannot resist? What place would there be for the whole of the Torah? Or by what justice and by what right could He punish the wicked or reward the righteous?" (Maimonides, *Mishneh Torah*, Hilchot Teshuvah V, 1 ff).

Plainly, this compels us to recognize ethical freedom as the very presupposition and basis of law and ethics. And as a result Judaism unequivocally teaches that man is absolutely and unconditionally free in his ethical choice of conduct. He is neither righteous nor wicked but is endowed to choose either path.

CHRISTIANITY, in contradistinction to Judaism, is predicated on the doctrine of "original sin" which implies the belief in ethical predestination. And thus while Judaism makes the Rabbinical benediction, "My God, the soul which Thou hast given me is pure" (Berachot 60b), part of the daily prayer, Christianity, in its authoritative Paulinian interpretation, teaches that every human being is tainted with the guilt of Adam and burdened with "original sin." According to Christian belief, man is ever dragged down to perdition by "original sin" whose weight is so powerful that he cannot liberate himself from its compulsion by his own ethical effort. In order to gain freedom from "original sin," a special act of "grace" is necessary, according to Christian belief. This act of "grace" was provided, so Christianity teaches, by Jesus' sacrificial death as atonement for the sins of mankind. As a result, Christianity does not recognize any other salvation or redemption from sin except belief in Jesus, and that he died to atone for the sins of mankind.

The differences between the Jewish and the Christian interpretation of sin has agitated not a few Christian theologicians and Bible scholars who, bound by Christian dogmas, maintain that the doctrine of "original sin" is superior to the Jewish creed of free will and the innate purity of every soul. This dissimilarity is usually emphasized by contrasting the Old Testament with the New Testament teachings. Thus the late Professor Toy wrote: "We must therefore regard the Old Testament as teaching not that sin is nature but that it is a tendency. It is described as a weakness, a failure, a violent outbreak, a perverseness, or as blindness and folly. It is a disposition or inclination which constantly impels or allures men to wrong-doing; it is not an utter incapacity to do right. It is an enemy ever present, watchful, alert, but not invincible; it can be overcome by man's own effort" (Toy, *Judaism and Christianity*, p.193).

With this Old Testament creed the Christian doctrine of sin is then compared: "Christianity, however, by emphasizing the sinfulness of sin, brought into sharper relief the moral feebleness of human nature and the necessity for the assistance and the sustaining grace of God. Paul, under the guidance of his dogmatic system went a step further, and formulated the doctrine of the natural man's incapacity to do good. In his view, the fatal religious error was the belief in obedience to law as the ground of salvation; the inability of obedience to save came to rest in his mind on man's inability to obey, and this inability involved or was identified with moral impotency. He represents the flesh—that is, normal human nature—as absolutely antagonistic in ethical tone and works to the divine spirit; each of these elements of life cherishes desires hostile to each other—they are contrary to each other" (*op. cit.*, pp. 212f).

Here another significant difference between Judaism and Christianity becomes apparent, namely, the Christian emphasis on the antagonism of the soul and "the flesh."

Christianity regards "the flesh" as the cause and the seat of original sin and therefore condemns the body as evil incarnate and as opposed and hostile to the spirit. Judaism, however, perceives no antagonism between body and soul but proclaims their harmony. For not "the flesh" is evil and wicked but only the unbridled concession to its desires. Consequently, Judaism does not regard the mortification and "crucifixion of the flesh" as a satisfactory solution of the moral problem. On the contrary, it holds that morality and ethics are inseparable from life in the flesh, and so it makes the care and sustenance of the body a sacred religious duty. We shall yet return to this theme in the chapter "Attitudes to Asceticism." Here we can only say that, together with the doctrine of "original sin," Judaism also rejects the notion that the body is inevitably and irrevocably the source and cause of sinfulness.

The Jewish creed is that the body, as well as the soul, is potentially pure. "Nothing in the human body is unclean; all of it is pure" (Sa'adya, Emunot VeDeot VI, 17).

As the presupposition and logical justification of Jesus' ministry and sacrificial death, the doctrine of "original sin" is basic and central in Christianity, and is accepted as a dogma by all Christian denominations and sects from the most orthodox to the most reformed. They hold that Adam's fall transmitted to all future generations of mankind, till Kingdom come, an inescapable burden of guilt, "original sin." This load descends on every human being in the very moment he leaves his mother's womb. There is no escape from "original sin," and no mortal can free himself from it by his own effort, according to Christian belief. It is only in "grace," that is to say, in the belief that God gave "His only begotten son" as a sacrifice for mankind's guilt, that the Christian sees the hope of escape from eternal perdition and damnation, the penalty for "original sin."

JUDAISM HAS NO ROOM for anything resembling the Christian doctrine of "original sin," for to the Jew this doctrine represents not only a negation of religion but also a denial of the possibility of ethics. In upholding freedom of the will, the medieval Jewish philosopher Joseph Albo correctly emphasized that Judaism opposes any infringement of this principle not merely from considerations of a specifically Jewish character, but because such a view is wrong and unethical (Ikkarim I, 9).

To be sure, Jews do not deny that sin exists; they refuse, however, to admit that it *must* exist, as Christians hold. The Torah recognizes that there is temptation and that "sin croucheth at the door; and unto thee is its desire." However, this memorable passage also emphasizes *"thou mayest rule over it"* (Genesis 4:7). And thus whereas Christianity teaches that *sin rules man*, Judaism declares that *man rules sin.* This, then, is the difference between the Jewish and the Christian doctrine of sin.

Judaism teaches that God created in man the good inclination *and* the evil inclination, for without *freedom to sin* there could be no *freedom to act righteously.* On the other hand, however, the "evil inclination" must not be permitted to become an irresistible compulsion, and so the Rabbis teach: "One should always stir up his good inclination against his evil inclination" (Berachot 5a).

A profusion of authoritative talmudic and medieval pronouncements, which are reiterated by modern Jewish thinkers and teachers, affirm that the sinful inclination and the temptation of sin *can* and *must* be ruled. The Jew is taught that the human soul is created pure and untainted. His hope is that at his death he may be as free from sin as he was at birth (Yerushalmi, Berachot 4d). The same thought is expressed in the rabbinic exhortation to return one's soul to its Maker in the same state of purity he received it as a trust (Shabbat 152b). Obviously, this leaves no loophole for anything *resembling* in the slightest the Christian dogma of "original sin."

The Christian seeks protection and escape from "original sin" and sinfulness in general under the wings of belief in "grace," as manifest in Jesus' career and sacrificial death. The Jew challenges sin proudly and defiantly, strengthened by the Divine pledge that he himself can subdue and rule it. Far from a curse or misfortune, Judaism regards the temptation of sin a precious and characteristic human distinction. For, "there is no evil inclination in animals" (Avot d'Rabbi Nathan XVI). The evil impulse, which must and can be mastered, is peculiar to man and adds to his worth and dignity rather than detracting from them. The Rabbis pithily interpreted the commandment: *And Thou shalt love the Lord thy God with all thy heart* (Deuteronomy 6:5) as implying that one should serve God with both impulses—the good inclination and the evil inclination (Sifri edited by Friedman, Deuteronomy #32; p. 73a). The same thought is expressed in the Midrashic exposition of the passage *And God saw everything that He had made and, behold it was very good* (Genesis 1:31). The expression *very good* is regarded as an allusion also to the evil inclination, for if not for that inclination, in its sublimated form, of course, nobody would build a house, marry, beget children, and engage in useful endeavor (Bereshit Rabba 9:7). The lesson to be deduced is that sexual desire and ambition for worldly success are not evil *per se* but only if they are gratified promiscuously and are not subjected to the control of the "good inclination."

Christian sacred literature abounds in narrations about "saints" who miraculously defeated the "devil." Judaism does not know a power of evil independent from and opposed to God. Jewish piety, therefore, is not tested in battles with the devil but in the very real and realistic struggle with the "evil impulse." There are numerous talmudic stories about Sages who subdued their sinful desires with the strong weapon of the "good impulse." These tales reflect zest and joyousness rather than resignation and sorrow. The Jew *rejoices* when he can prove his ethical mettle in the *unaided* battle against the temptations of sin. For without temptation and its powerful lure there would be no merit in resisting it. This attitude is strikingly expressed in the talmudic story about the pious Rabbi Amram's duel with sensual desire:

Once, feeling himself incapable to resist the temptation of a beautiful woman, the Rabbi sought safety in numbers and summoned his colleagues with the cry: "Amram's house is on fire." But they could not extinguish the blaze of the passion that threatened to consume him. Then Rabbi Amram himself drove out the sinful desire from his heart and when it went forth from him like a pillar of fire, he taunted it: "Although you are fire and I flesh—yet I am stronger than you!" (Kiddushin 81a).

The Jew is taught to regard himself always and ever as *stronger* than sin and the power that draws him to it. He is bidden to glory in that strength, in the manner Rabbi Amram did. And so, even when he succumbs to sin, the Jew still knows that if he only tries hard enough, he can defeat the evil impulse. Although sinful desire is fire, man is stronger than it; he can extinguish it with his ethical impulse.

"I am stronger than you!" This is the Jewish answer to sin, and Jews therefore have never resorted to any other weapon against the evil inclination except the good impulse and the power of ethical choice.

OBVIOUSLY, this view is strongly dynamic, in contradistinction to the static Christian dogmas of "original sin" and "grace." The dynamic spirit of Judaism makes it incumbent upon its confessors to strive incessantly for greater ethical perfection through the subjugation of the evil instinct. The desired perfection is boundless, and so the Jew must ever exert himself in renewed ethical efforts. He cannot relax and rest during the climb toward the ethical heights he is bidden to scale and rely upon a "savior" to carry him on high. He himself must trace the difficult road, slowly and step by step—for were it otherwise, there would be no merit in piety and no glory and triumph in the defeat of the "evil impulse."

The ethical problem confronting the believing Christian is simpler and less challenging. He is first of all required to believe in Jesus and that he died for mankind's sins. This belief, and nothing else, opens wide the gates of the Christian Paradise. Of course, the Christian, too, is bidden to lead a virtuous life. The fact, however, remains that Christianity places "grace" above conduct and ethical effort in the successful quest for salvation. Christianity does not appreciate the exhilarating ethical stimulation of the challenge of the "evil impulse," for it regards sin not as a *challenge* but as the inescapable *fate* of every human being from which there is only one deliverance: the "grace" of Jesus' sacrificial death. Christians, therefore, sometimes find it difficult to appreciate the Jewish regard for the man who "turned away from the sin whose taste he knew, and subdued his evil impulse" (Maimonides, Hilchot Teshuvah VII, 4). Here, again, the dynamic element of ethical progress is exalted above ethical perfection attained by mere passive belief.

The dynamic character of Jewish ethics is perhaps most memorably glorified in the following pithy talmudic allegory: "In the world-to-come the Holy One, blessed be He, will bring the evil inclination and slay it before the righteous and the wicked. To the righteous it will seem like a mighty mountain, but to the wicked like a single hair. Both will weep. The righteous will weep and exclaim: 'How could we conquer such a high mountain as this?' And the wicked will weep and say: 'How is it that we could not subdue a single hair like this?'" (Sukkah 52a).

This, then, is the reward of piety and the penalty of sin: the ethical victory of the righteous is aggrandized and projected into such dimensions that those who won it are shocked at its magnitude. The punishment of the sinners, on the other hand, consists in the minimization of the challenge they failed to meet successfully, so that they are confounded in shame for having been unable to subdue that "single hair."

There is no bridge that could span the gulf separating the Jewish doctrines of free will and freedom of ethical choice from the Christian dogmas of "original sin" and "grace."

CHAPTER IV

Sin
and Atonement

THE CHRISTIAN DOCTRINES of "original sin" and of the "corruption of the flesh" lead to the conclusion of man's incapacity to atone unaided for his staggering load of guilt. This distrust in the efficacy of the ethical effort *per se* inevitably induces doubts in the adequacy of repentance as the medium of the sinner's reconciliation with God. And so Christianity teaches that repentance and the mending of one's ways do not suffice for procuring Divine forgiveness. Man is so deeply immersed in guilt, his own and the hereditary sin of the human race, that he cannot hope to extricate himself from this mire of perdition without the assistance of "grace."

Christianity postulates that this saving act of grace is supplied by Jesus' "vicarious atonement." Knowing the insufficiency of the moral resources of the sinner, God sacrificed "His Only Begotten Son" to atone for the sins of mankind. To quote Professor Toy: "We may sum up Paul's doctrine of saving righteousness as follows: its legal condition is the sacrificial death of Jesus Christ; its ethical content is the personal righteousness of Christ; its source is the power of the living, glorified Christ committed to him by God and exercised through the spirit; its human condition is the humble and grateful recognition of Jesus as the perfect ideal, through whose presence the soul is transformed" (Toy, *Judaism and Christianity*, p. 281). The Christian therefore attains forgiveness "in accepting Jesus Christ" (*op. cit.*, 275) and by acknowledging that Jesus died also for *his* (the sinner's) transgressions.

The idea of "vicarious atonement," that is to say, the payment of the penalty not by the sinner but by a substitute, is irreconcilable with Jewish ethics. Judaism exalts justice as one of the foundations of the universe. It is unjust, and inconsistent as well, to sacrifice a perfectly innocent "Savior" for the transgressions of the sinners. It is inconsistent and unjust, for justice requires that the sinner bear the consequences of his actions.

The Pentateuch records that when the Lord threatened to punish Israel for the heinous sin of worshipping the "Golden Calf," Moses petitioned God as follows: "Oh, this people have sinned a great sin, and have made a god of gold. Yet now, if thou wilt forgive their sin—; and if not, blot me, I pray Thee, out of Thy book which Thou hast written." To this plea God replied: "Whosoever hath sinned against Me, him will I blot out of My book" (Exodus 32:32f). In other words, Moses cannot atone for the sins of the Israelites; they themselves must bear the penalty. For justice requires that *"whosoever hath sinned"* shall suffer.

The idea of the ethical justification of punishment for the sinner was further elaborated and refined by the Prophets, especially Jeremiah and Ezekiel, who vigorously attacked the popular notion that God punishes men for sins other than their own. "Everyone shall die for his own iniquity" proclaims Jeremiah (31:30). In the same vein Ezekiel chides his contemporaries steeped in mythological superstitions: "What mean ye, that ye use this proverb in the land of Israel, saying: 'The fathers have eaten sour grapes, and the children's teeth are set on edge?' As I live, saith the Lord God, ye shall not have occasion any more to use this proverb in Israel. Behold, all souls are Mine; as the soul of the father, so also the soul of the son is Mine; the soul that sinneth, it shall die" (18:2f).

The soul that sinneth it shall die. This is the voice of reason and of justice and the watchword of Judaism. "Vicarious atonement" is therefore inacceptable to the Jew; the Christian, on the other hand, regards it as the choicest fruit of his religion. Can these two diametrically opposed views be reconciled?

The negative Jewish attitude to any semblance even of "vicarious atonement" is strikingly illustrated by a story in the "Book of the Pious," telling about a chasid who voluntarily assumed special hardships because he was troubled by the Midrashic exposition of Isaiah's prophecy of the "Suffering Servant" (chapter 53) which pictures the Messiah as "wounded for our transgression." When a disciple asked the chasid why he took upon himself such severe penances, he replied: "I do not want anyone but myself to suffer for my sins" (*Sefer Chasidim*, ed. Wistinetzki, No. 1556).

The doctrine of "vicarious atonement" quite logically led to the belief in Jesus' role as the mediator between men and their Father in Heaven. Judaism, on the other hand, being irrevocably committed to the conviction that each and every human being has always and ever access to God, provided he draws near to Him in truth and righteousness, rejects the very ideas of mediation, for man can approach God through prayer, and hope to be heard. God is as close to *every* person as he wants to be to God. And *every* one therefore can *know* God to the fullest possible extent.

Judaism is essentially democratic. As a result, it has never sanctioned doctrines implying an affirmation of the *in*equality of men before God. Before God all men are equal, and there is no need, therefore, for mediation by a Savior.

Here, then, is another major difference between Judaism and Christianity: whereas Judaism avows that God is near to every man, nearer, in fact, than any nearness we can imagine, Christianity teaches that God is eternally distant and removed from man, who can enter a correlation with Him solely and exclusively through the mediation of Jesus, the "Son of God." Again, it would be futile to argue that Protestantism, which recognizes solely the mediation of the "Son of God" but not that of Mary, the Saints and of the priesthood, is closer to Judaism than Catholicism which, besides the mediation of Jesus, stresses also these other agents of mediation. The difference, again, is one of quantity only. Yet even the *quantity* of the difference between Judaism, which categorically rejects *any* mediation between man and God, and Protestantism, which acknowledges it unreservedly in the case of Jesus, is such that it is no less unbridgeable than the very *quality* of that contradistinction.

Christianity is irrevocably committed to all that is implied in Jesus' teaching: "Nor does anyone know the Father except the Son and to whom the Son deigns to reveal Him" (Matthew 11:27). That is to say, the knowledge of God, the birthright of every human being, according to Jewish conviction, is denied to man under the Christian dispensation, for that knowledge is not the reward of individual effort but the gift of arbitrary grace; it will only be given to him to whom the Son deigns to reveal it.

Judaism, thanks to its democratic impetus, is committed to the hope that all human beings will eventually attain to the knowledge of God through their own effort; all men, and not only those to whom the Son chooses to impart this knowledge. The Jewish eagerness to share the highest degree of spiritual illumination with all human beings is gloriously revealed in the Biblical narrative of Eldad and Medad, who prophesied without authorization. When Joshua requested Moses to silence their voices, he replied: "Art thou jealous for my sake? Would that all the Lord's people were prophets, that the Lord would put His spirit upon them" (Numbers 11:29).

Would that all the Lord's people were prophets! This is the democratic ideal to which Judaism has adhered since its very inception. Obviously, this democratization of the sublimest spiritual attainment cannot be harmonized with the Christian dogma of "grace" through the mediation of a Savior.

The uncompromising Jewish attitude to mediation in the religious sphere is strikingly illustrated in a rabbinic discussion of the Pentateuchal institution of the priestly blessing. Although the priestly benediction stresses that all blessings flow from God ("The Lord bless thee, and keep thee, the Lord make His face to shine upon thee, and give thee peace"), the Rabbis emphasized that the priests have no power to bless— they only enunciate the formula, but the blessing comes from God. According to an ancient Midrash the Israelites, dismayed when God commanded Aaron and his sons to bless the community (Numbers 6:22–27), exclaimed: "Master of the Universe, You tell the priests to bless us—but we need only Your blessing." And God pacified their qualms, "Although I commanded the priests to bless you, I am with them to bless you" (Bemidbar Rabba XI:2). Another comment on the Divine promise "and I will bless them," in the same Midrashic homily, stresses that this declaration makes it clear that the priests have no power to bless or to withhold the blessing. They are only the mouthpieces of God, Who is the only source of blessing (Bemidbar Rabba XI:8).

The rejection of even the slightest vestige of mediation or intercession eventually gave rise to one of the loftiest ethical ideas: the conviction that redemption from sin is fully within the sinner's power. All he need do to be forgiven is repent sincerely. Repentance (*teshuvah*, literally "return") atones for his transgressions and thus effects the reconciliation with God.

The sinner requires no outside help or intercession to obtain Divine forgiveness. All that is asked of him is that he "return" from his evil ways and practice the righteousness God has decreed for him. Because man is endowed with "free will," and not weighed down by hereditary sin or irresistible wickedness, he has always and ever the possibility to "return" by means of his own ethical resources and efforts.

The difference between atonement through grace and atonement through autonomous ethical effort is usually stressed in Christian attempts to demonstrate the preeminence and advantages of "vicarious atonement" over autonomous atonement and forgiveness, as demanded by Judaism. Thus Dr. A. Lukyn Williams writes: "To the Jew the subject of reconciliation with God presents no doctrinal difficulty. He holds that however many and gross his sins may be he has only to repent sincerely, with all his heart and soul, and his Father in heaven forgives him completely, and restores him to his proper condition of full sonship.

"To the Christian the case stands quite otherwise. His opinion about sin and its awfulness—far deeper than the al most superficial acknowledgment by Jews of separate sins— compels him to require not only repentance on the part of the sinner, but an action outside the sinner himself which corresponds to his sin.

"The Christian holds that his sin must be met in some way, and that mere forgiveness by God is not sufficient in itself. Mere forgiveness of sin seems to be immoral" (*The Doctrines of Modern Judaism Considered*, 1939, p. 159).

The suggestion that "mere forgiveness of sin seems to be immoral" is inevitably incomprehensible to Jews, who are nurtured in the conviction that repentance and forgiveness constitute the only legitimate ethical instruments for annulling sin.

"The Christian solution," on the other hand, is, as Dr. Williams elaborates, that "the One and Only God, in His manifestation of Himself (i.e., Jesus) . . . submitted to every form of indignity, even to Death itself. . . . Sin has its logical issue in Death, and only by voluntarily enduring Death, without sin, can the sacrifice be complete, and the Atonement perfect in the eyes of the moral sense of the universe" (*op. cit.,* p. 160). Judaism cannot follow her daughter religion on this flight into the realms of mythology. It cannot understand why an "innocent sacrifice" is required to atone for the guilt of the sinner. To Christians, however, such a substitution seems perfectly in order. And so Dr. Williams, scanning the horizon of world religions for solutions of the problem of sin, concludes that there is only "one method" by which it can be defeated, namely, "God's own self-sacrifice. Nor did God shrink even from this. He, in the full manifestation of Himself (i.e., Jesus) . . . did thus show by His own act the exceeding sinfulness of sin and by this supreme self-sacrifice purify all creation, including the highest heavens, from the stain of sin and at last from its very presence" (*op. cit.,* p. 161).

Mature Judaism requires no sacrifice from either God or man for the purification of the sinner, for "the gates of repentance" are always open and God is ever ready to receive the returning sinner. All Jewish sources sound in endless variations and scales the call to repentance, holding out the promise and the assurance of forgiveness to all those who sincerely repent having strayed from the path of righteousness:

> Let the wicked forsake his way,
> And the man of iniquity his thoughts;
> And let him return unto the Lord,
> And He will have compassion upon him
> And to our God, for he will abundantly pardon.
> (Isaiah 55:7)

In the same vein the Prophet Ezekiel promises: "But if the wicked turn from all his sins that he hath committed, and keep all My statutes, and do that which is lawful and right, he shall surely live, he shall not die. None of his transgressions that he hath committed shall be remembered against him; for his righteousness that he hath done he shall live. Have I any pleasure at all that the wicked should die? saith the Lord; and not rather that he should return from his ways, and live?" (18:21–23). And again, "Return ye, and turn yourselves from all your transgressions; so shall they not be a stumbling block of iniquity unto you. Cast away from you all your transgressions, wherein you have transgressed; and make you a new heart and a new spirit" (Ezekiel 18:30f).

The *making* of the new heart and of the new spirit, this is what Judaism requires of the sinner. Forgiveness is predicated on ethical regeneration, and salvation can only be procured through unremitting efforts of mending one's ways. According to Jewish conviction, there are no intercessors other than "repentance and good deeds" (Shabbat 32a).

Sacrifices, prayers and even the Day of Atonement cannot annul man's sin; his own *teshuvah*, his own repentance and ethical effort of regeneration are demanded. No matter how grave the transgression, sincere repentance atones for it, for "there is nothing greater than repentance" (Devarim Rabba II, 24). What Judaism means by true repentance may be seen from Rabbi Judah's opinion that the true penitent is he "who when the same opportunity for sin presents itself once or twice refrains from sinning, although it is the same woman, the same time, the same place" (Yoma 86b). It is not words, or even belief, that count in repentance but solely the right spirit and the right action. Consequently, the Elders would admonish the people on fast days: "It is not said of the people of Nineveh, *And God saw their sackcloth and their fasting,* but *And God saw their works, that they turned from their evil way"* (Jonah 3:10; Taanit II, 1).

THERE ARE no bounds to the efficacy of repentance. No power on earth or in heaven can frustrate it. "Even if one has been wicked all one's life and repents in the end, his sin is not remembered against him" (Kiddushin 40b). But "he who says: I shall sin and then repent, I shall sin and the Day of Atonement will procure forgiveness" (Yoma VIII, 9) will not be granted forgiveness. It is instructive to compare this Mishnaic teaching with an excerpt from one of Martin Luther's letters to Melanchthon: "Sin more strongly but be stronger in faith and rejoice in Christ, who is the victor of sin, death and the world. We must sin, as long as we are here. . . It is enough if through the riches of God's glory we recognize the Lamb of God which takes away the sins of the world; from Him sin will not tear us away even if thousands upon thousands of times daily we commit fornication and murder" (Paul Goodman, *The Synagogue and the Church*, p. 360). And again, "Now you see how rich the Christian is: even if he wishes he cannot lose his salvation, however great his sins may be, unless he does not desire to believe. No sin can damn him, except want of faith" (*op. cit.*, p. 359).

According to Jewish conviction belief is no safeguard of ethics nor a cure for sin. Judaism knows only one antidote against sin: repentance coupled with righteous conduct. In keeping with this, Rabbi Eliezer taught: "Repent one day before your death." And when his pupils rejoined that this was impossible since no one knows his day of death, the Sage replied: "How much more reason then to repent today, lest he be dead tomorrow. Thus, all one's days will be spent in repentance" (Shabbat 153a).

In comparing "Christian love" with "Jewish legalism" Christian authors invariably emphasize the miracle of Divine love manifest in the Lord's sacrifice of His "Son" so that sinful men may attain salvation. They glory in the Divine "grace" thus bestowed upon all believers in Christ and deplore the fact that the Jews reject this saving "love" and "grace." In fact, however, "grace" is not at all unknown to Judaism. The sacred Jewish writings abound in attestations of God's love for mankind and of His lovingkindness and the "grace" manifest in His merciful forgiveness. Judaism assuredly knows "love" and "grace." However while Christianity makes Jesus the embodiment of "love" and "grace" and commands the believers to seek Divine grace through his mediation, Judaism has consistently maintained that the abundance of love and of grace are within reach of all in the nearness to God Himself.

According to Jewish belief God alone forgives sins. As He is all-powerful and His mercy limitless, the repentant sinner is assured of the fullness of grace and the abundance of Divine love and forgiveness. "If your sins reach unto heaven, even unto the seventh heaven, and even to the Throne of Glory, and you repent, I will accept you," is God's pledge to the sinners. Is a higher degree of "love" and "grace" possible?

The Rabbis took special pains to stress that no matter how deep the sinners may have sunk, they are not lost. Repentance can save them and restore their souls. "Let not the sinner say, there is no reinstatement for me. Instead, let him trust in God and repent—and God will receive him" (Midrash Tehilim, edited by Buber 129a; on Psalm 49:4). Another beautiful rabbinic passage represents God as saying that "if someone would say that God does not accept the penitents, Manasseh (the wicked king of Israel) would come and testify against him, for there was never anybody more sinful than he, and yet, in the hour of his repentance, I received him, as it is said: 'And

he prayed unto Him; and He was entreated of him'"
(Bemidbar Rabba XIV, 1). And again, "God says: My hands
are stretched out to the repentant sinner: I reject no one who
turns His heart to Me in repentance" (Midrash Tehilim, edited by Buber 253a; on Psalm 120:7).

The merit of the repentance of the wicked exceeds even
that of the prayer of the most righteous. Thus "Moses' prayer
to enter Eretz Israel was not granted, but the repentance of
Rahab the harlot was accepted" (*Seder Eliahu Zuta*, edited by
Friedman, p. 37). According to the Rabbis repentance is
among the seven things whose creation preceded that of the
universe (Pesachim 54a). It is the only effective means of reconciliation with God. Rabbi Akiba therefore proudly proclaimed: "Happy are you, O Israelites! Before whom do you
cleanse yourselves from sin, and who purges you? Your Father in heaven!" (Yoma VIII, 9).

God and the repentant sinner are thus brought together
in the ethical and purely spiritual correlation of repentance
and forgiveness. Every sinner is capable and therefore obliged
to approach God in contrition and remorse and with the
determination of ethical regeneration.

No bridge leads from this dynamic interpretation of sin
and atonement to the essentially static Christian doctrine of
"vicarious atonement" which negates the Jewish convictions
of man's unqualified freedom in the ethical sphere and his
power to attain forgiveness without the help of an interces-
sor or savior.

CHAPTER V

Attitudes and Asceticism

J UDAISM IS INDIGENOUSLY OPTIMISTIC. Affirming a benefi-
cent Creator, it regards the world and all that fills it as "very
good." God, however, did not only create the soul but also
formed the "flesh" and its desires. Judaism therefore does not
condemn the "flesh" as wicked, nor does it postulate an irreconcilable antithesis between the "flesh" and the "spirit." It
sees harmony everywhere and accepts the physical and the
spiritual as equally important to the harmonious development
of the personality. Jews do not deprecate the "flesh" and its
needs in favor of the "spirit." Their wholesome acceptance of
reality prevents them from seeing a conflict between body and
soul. God formed the body and He created the soul; consequently, the physical urges and desires cannot be bad.

Nor does Judaism decry the "flesh" as the seat of the "baser
instincts" and as the source of all evil. As a result, pessimistic
asceticism is utterly foreign to the Jewish psychology. Judaism accepts the "flesh" as the handiwork of God and therefore regards it as no less sacred than the soul. Matter and spirit
complement one another; since the one cannot exist without
the other, it would be sheer folly to despise and degrade the

body through which the spirit must manifest itself. Besides, it would be tantamount to rebellion against God Who created man as an inseparable union of the physical and the spiritual, of body and soul.

Judaism therefore accepts the body, its needs and its desires not grudgingly and with misgivings but with glad affirmation. Of course, there is a distinct difference between the transitory goodness of the physical and the eternal goodness of the things of the spirit; however, this does not imply that the transitory is base and wicked. The Jew strives toward the spiritualization of matter, but simultaneously he is sufficiently realistic to know that the ideal can be realized only in and through matter. Consequently, it would be absurd to despise the vessel which holds the precious substance.

Instead of deprecating the "animal instincts," Judaism attempts to transvaluate them in accordance with their sublime ethical potentialities. The ideal of Jewish saintliness is not realized by the ascete who has "purged" himself from all fleshly desires but, on the contrary, by him in whom those desires burn fiercest and yet, without being altogether starved, are tamed and governed. There is a remarkable talmudic statement to the effect that the greater the personality the more intense his animal desires (Sukkah 52a), that is to say, the more consuming and powerful are his passions. The Sages who perceived this interdependence of intellectual creativeness and physical desire anticipated Freud's psychoanalytical theories of the libido and the cultural potentialities of the sublimated sexual instinct by two thousand years. . . . The creative personality is almost invariably "over-sexed." While the undisciplined, however, let their sex-glands get the best of them, the disciplined genius "sublimates" the overabundance of libido, translating it into cultural energy. It is therefore not the "animal instinct" that leads to grief but the failure to harness and sublimate it.

This wholesome attitude to the body and the ready acceptance of the "animal instincts" rendered impossible the development of any type of asceticism within Judaism. Jews have never regarded the mortification of the flesh as pious. The fact that God created the good things of the earth is accepted as cogent proof that these blessings are to be enjoyed. Jewish piety does not consist in fasting, celibacy, solitude and other ascetic deprivations contrary to human nature and God's purpose. To the Jew abstinence of any kind is outright sinful, for it bespeaks the rejection of the good things created by God's bounty. The Sages even threatened that in the world-to-come man will have to account for every legitimate enjoyment he denied himself (Yerushalmi Kiddushin IV, end). In the same spirit they interpreted the "sin-offering" the Nazarite was required to bring at the end of his term (Numbers 6:13f) as expiation for his vow of abstention by which he sinned against his own person (Nedarim 10a). They concluded that if the Nazarite, who abstained only from wine, needed atonement, how much more he who abstains from all pleasurable things (Sifri, Naso #30, edited by Friedman, p. 10a).

Far from being meritorious, it is sinful to weaken the body by ascetic practices detrimental to health. The care of the body and the preservation of health are insistently enjoined by Jewish law. According to Maimonides, who as a physician felt especially keen about this point, one acts piously by keeping the body healthy and strong. For "since it is impossible to have any understanding and knowledge of the Creator when one is sick, it is man's duty to avoid whatever is injurious to the body and cultivate habits that promote health and vigor" (Hilchot Deot IV, 1).

One of the best summations of the Jewish attitude to asceticism comes from the poet-philosopher Yehudah Halevi, who asserted in his *Kuzari* that "a servant of God is not he who withdraws from the world . . . or hates life which is one of God's good gifts. . . . On the contrary, he loves the world and long life, because it offers him opportunities to earn the world-to-come" (*Kuzari* III, 1).

Jewish love of life, however, is not synonymous with unbridled hedonism. The two extremes of asceticism and of undisciplined indulgence are rejected. Instead the ideal of training the physical desires to "obedience" is advanced (*Kuzari* III, 5). Desire must be ruled by reason and ethics and blend into a harmonious and wholesome union of the physical and the spiritual. The pious will not afflict his body with deprivations but will satisfy all its needs in moderation and propriety. He will, to quote from Maimonides' regimen of the scholar and gentleman, "not be a glutton but will eat sufficiently to sustain his body with healthful food. . . . He will not be eager to stuff his stomach like those who gorge themselves with food and drink. . . . " Also, he will not be addicted to the cup, for "he who drinks to intoxication is a sinner and despicable; and he jeopardizes his wisdom. . . ." (Hilchot Deot V, 3). As to the pleasures of love, the scholar and gentleman governs his desires. He will not indulge in promiscuous licentiousness but will be faithful and devoted to his wife. In short, the Torah wants men to follow in moderation the dictates of nature: to eat, drink, love and take their places in society, honestly and righteously, but not to torture themselves with ascetic practices (Maimonides, Shemoneh Perakim IV).

Despite these injunctions against asceticism, there arose minor and sporadic ascetic movements within Judaism. If invariably they were nipped in the bud, it was because the people adhered to the common sense teachings of their Rabbis who taught that the prohibitions of the Torah must not be augmented arbitrarily.

Judaism advocates the "golden mean." One must not be a glutton and make eating the purpose of life, nor must one stumble into the other extreme and impose upon oneself fasts, for, according to the Sages, "he who makes a habit of fasting is a sinner" (Nedarim 10a). The weakening of the body through fasts impairs also the faculties of the mind. Far from promoting spirituality, therefore, fasting really retards and arrests it. The scholars and teachers especially are warned against excessive fasting, for the hardship inevitably impairs their pedagogic efficiency.

THE FACT that "innocence" is a colloquial synonym for "virginity" reveals to what extent the popular mind identifies sex with sin. This attitude is the result of the New Testament disparagement of marriage as a necessary evil for the propagation of the race and the glorification of celibacy as the higher ideal.

To the Jew celibacy is not only unnatural but definitely contrary to the will of God Who commanded man and woman to be fruitful and multiply and Who created the earth "not a waste; He formed it to be inhabited" (Isaiah 45:18). Marriage, therefore, is not a necessary evil but the joyful consummation of the human destiny. Western man, as a result of the Christian teachings of the wickedness of sex, has only lately dared to assert openly the legitimacy of the joy of love, besides and above its procreative purpose. The Jews never doubted its legitimacy, for, according to the Rabbis, he who is unmarried lives "without joy, without blessing, without goodness" (Yevamot 62b). Apart, man and woman are incomplete for "the human being is man and his wife."

Jews have always been remarkably uninhibited. The Sages discussed the intimate aspects of marriage with the same candid objectivity as the legal details of a real estate transaction. Sex is not "a forbidden topic" to the Jew—it is part of life and consequently good and clean. There was nothing puritanical about the great Jewish teachers of all ages. They did not shut their eyes to the sexual problem but tackled it freely and intelligently, with the result that sexual morality among Jews has been uniformly high. The fact that Jewish law stresses the joy of love, besides its procreative purpose, and urges man and his wife to drain freely, yet with moderation, the cup of physical love has proved a powerful antidote against sexual hypocrisy and puritanism.

Christianity, in contradistinction to Judaism's joyous affirmation of marriage and love, disparages the "flesh" as the source of all evil and, consequently, glorifies celibacy. And so "they that are of Christ Jesus have crucified the flesh with its passions and desires" (Galatians 5:24). The irreconcilable difference between Judaism and Christianity is accentuated by the New Testament juxtaposition of the "spirit" and the "flesh" which negates the Jewish optimism and its wholesome acceptance of the body as the medium of expression for the spirit. And so while all Jewish sources consistently teach the *mitzvah* of the lawful satisfaction of the physical needs, the New Testament demands: "Live by the spirit, and then you will not indulge your physical cravings. For the physical cravings are against the spirit, and the cravings of the spirit are against the physical; the two are in opposition" (Galatians 5:16ff).

The logical conclusion of this disparagement of the "flesh" was the proclamation of celibacy as the ideal for the higher, spiritual man, who should make himself a "eunuch for the kingdom of heaven's sake" (Matthew 19:12), an ideal that is still adhered to by the Catholic priesthood and the members of Catholic religious orders. While all Jewish teachings exalt marriage as sacred, Jesus disparaged it in dire severity, for he held that only "the people of this world marry and are married, but those that are thought worthy to attain the other world and the resurrection from the dead, neither marry, nor are married" (Luke, 20:34–35). The same spirit motivates Paul's instruction to the Corinthians: "To all who are unmarried and to widows, I would say this: it is an excellent thing if they can remain single as I am, but if they cannot control themselves, let them marry. For it is better to marry than to be on fire with passion" (I Corinthians 7:9). At best, therefore, New Testament Christianity regards marriage as a concession to the "flesh" and its consuming fire, a view that is utterly incompatible with Judaism, which prescribes a special marriage benediction rendering thanks unto God "Who causes the bridegroom to rejoice with his bride."

Although Protestantism has abolished celibacy, it still retains the sense of "sexual guilt" inevitably engendered by the New Testament disparagement of marriage.

POVERTY, glorified by Christianity as a sacred and desirable state, appears to the realistic view of Judaism as a stumbling block rather than a stimulus to piety. "Dire poverty leads man to sin against his Maker." Poverty is bad, for it compels one to devote the time that should be given to study and contemplation to the effort of toiling for one's daily bread. The life of the pauper is no life at all, for "poverty in the house is worse than fifty plagues" (Bava Batra 116a).

Since poverty is onerous and may easily prove a hindrance to piety, Judaism makes the proper care of one's possessions a religious obligation. The prohibition, "Thou shalt not destroy," applies also to squandering one's means. Of course, one must share with those less fortunate, but only *share* and not give them all one has. Maimonides in his "Letter to the Jews of Yemen" warns insistently against the folly of giving away all one owns. He takes the fact that the false messiah, who disturbed the peace of the South-Arabian Jewish communities in the eleventh century and against whom his "Epistle" was directed, demanded that his followers impoverish themselves, as proof of the man's unbalanced mind.

Judaism regards private property as legitimate and desirable. The ideal of poverty is other-worldly and unrealistic. It is the result of the mistaken notion that wealth is bad and despicable because some rich people misuse it. The Jewish view is that wealth is more conducive to piety and ethics than poverty, for only when one's physical needs are provided for can one concentrate upon the higher spheres of religion and ethics.

In contradistinction to this sanguine acceptance of the well-earned fruit of labor is Christianity's summary condemnation of the rich and the unqualified exaltation of the poor. Wealth and poverty are to Christianity not so much economic than moral states, the former all wicked and the latter all righteous. The Catholic Church therefore demands that the priests and the members of religious orders take the vow of poverty.

This summary condemnation of the rich and adulation of the poor has its roots in the New Testament, which abounds in such passages as, "it is easier for a camel to go through the eye of a needle than for a rich man to enter the kingdom of heaven" (Matthew 19:23).

Jesus' disciples, confused by this statement, which is contrary to the Jewish tradition in which they had been raised, asked him in dismay: "Here we have left all we had and followed you. What are we to have?" (Matthew 19:27). To which Jesus replied, again in a manner utterly irreconcilable with Jewish tenets and principles: "Anyone who has given up houses or brothers or sisters or father or mother or children or land for my sake will receive many times as much, and share eternal life" (Matthew 19:29). The flight from the world and, especially, from the members of one's family to whom one owes respect, honor and fealty is no mark of Jewish piety, but, on the contrary, a violation of the commandment "honor thy father and thy mother . . . ," which according to the rabbinic interpretation applies not merely to the parents but to all blood relations on the father's and the mother's side as well. Judaism sees no merit in abandoning one's houses and fields, giving them over to neglect in order to follow the promise of a "kingdom that is not of this world." To be sure, in the writings of the Prophets we find not a few condemnations of those who increase their riches by unrighteousness and the oppression and exploitation of the poor. But in the Hebrew Bible there is no statement to the effect that houses, fields and other possessions are in themselves bad and wicked. In the New Testament, however, we read: "Blessed are you who are poor, for the Kingdom of God is yours . . ." (Luke 6:20). And the antithesis: "Alas for you who are rich, for you have had your comfort! Alas for you have plenty to eat now, for you will be hungry" (Luke 6:24f). The fact that one can be rich and pious, or poor and impious, did not dawn upon the New Testament authors apparently. The Hebrew Bible, however, offers a multitude of instances, from Abraham to Job, proving that wealth does not only not constitute the negation of piety, but, on the contrary, is one of its desirable rewards.

The Christian equation of poverty and piety on the one hand and of wealth and impiety on the other is most graphically illustrated by Jesus' parable of Lazarus and the rich man:

> There was once a rich man, who used to dress in purple and fine linen, and to live in luxury every day. And a beggar named Lazarus was put down at his gate covered with sores and eager to satisfy his hunger with what was thrown from the rich man's table. Why, the very dogs came and licked his sores. And it came about that the beggar died and was carried away by the angels to the companionship of Abraham, and the rich man too died and was buried. And in Hell he looked up, tormented as he was, and saw Abraham far away, with Lazarus beside him. And he called to him and said: 'Father Abraham, take pity on me, and send Lazarus to dip the tip of his finger in water and

cool my tongue, for I am in torment, here in the flames!' And
Abraham said: 'My child, remember that you received your
blessings in your lifetime, and Lazarus had his misfortunes in
his; and now he is being comforted here, while you are in
anguish' (Luke 16:19–26).

To the Jew this parable is replete with glaring contradictions: why should the rich man suffer in hell when he did not
sin to deserve these tortures; and why should Lazarus enjoy
heavenly bliss when his "merit" was nothing else but his poverty and afflictions? But it also justifies unmerciful vengeance.
The rich man, in the throes of the agonies of hell, pleads for
pity and a drop of water; and Father Abraham, as represented
by Jesus, refuses to succor the rich man for no other or better
reason than that he already received his share of blessings. Is
this sufficient cause for eternal damnation and the refusal of
a drop of water? To the Jew, who is taught that piety and reward, and wickedness and punishment, stand in a causal
nexus, but not that poverty *is* piety and wealth *is* wickedness,
the Lazarus parable is an enigma.

We shall yet have occasion to dwell on the alleged differences between "Judaism, the religion of stern law," and "Christianity, the religion of merciful love." Here it is in place,
however, to point out that the New Testament attitude to the
rich man in the Lazarus parable is, from the Jewish point of
view, outright merciless—for how dare one refuse *pity* to the
sufferers? Judaism has never refused *pity* to anyone. Talmudic law provides that those condemned to death are to be given
a cup of wine with narcotic spices in order to make the ex-
ecution less painful. This was to be done for pity's sake.

The Lazarus parable, however, refuses even the small comfort of a drop of water to the rich man. And it represents the
tortures of hell which he endures as sort of a vengeance ex-
acted for the pleasures and the ease he enjoyed in life.

The Lazarus parable proves to what results the summary condemnation of wealth and the unqualified glorification of poverty may lead. Judaism avoided these extremes by joyfully and gratefully accepting material blessings as conducive to piety and godliness.

THE ETHICS of Judaism is social, and not individualistic. Little is gained for the progress of the world if one person achieves perfection and holiness. The Messianic ideal is that *all* nations and *all* individuals shall know peace, justice and neighborly love. Consequently, the "saint" who withdraws as a hermit from the community does not a thing to bring nearer the Messianic age. Jewish piety is not tested away from the turmoil of life but in the heat of its battle; sharing communal responsibility and rendering communal service are among its true marks, for Judaism decrees, "Do not segregate yourself from the community." Man can fulfill his purpose in life only as a member of the human family—never in solitude, which is contrary to human psychology and detrimental to the realization of ethics in society. The monastic hermit who withdraws from the world is therefore a sinner, according to the consensus of all Jewish teachers. He offends against the all-important commandment "love your neighbor as yourself," a commandment which one can only fulfill if he takes his place in the community, ready to share the joy and sorrow, the labor and the blessings of his fellow-men and letting them, in turn, share one's happiness and sorrow, too.

Christianity, especially in its Catholic interpretation, regards solitude as a desirable state of piety. The Christian conviction, contrary to that of Judaism, is that true piety flowers most luxuriously in monastic solitude. Accordingly, devout Catholics regard the convent as the abode of true godliness, where the pious monks and nuns, free from all mundane interests and concerns, can realize the Christian ideal of the renunciation of the "flesh." The would-be monk or nun must renounce the world in its entirety—even his closest blood relations—for true Christian piety can only be achieved—so the New Testament teaches insistently—in withdrawing from the world.

Although Protestantism has discarded the monastic ideal, its religious mood is still profoundly affected and moulded by the monastic tradition which regards solitary gloom as more conducive to religiosity than communal joy. This influence is especially marked in the puritanical trends of Calvinistic Protestantism.

JUDAISM is a joyous religion. Joy, and the optimism flowing from it, are its dominant notes. It has been correctly remarked that no other language boasts so many synonyms for "joy" as Hebrew. The Sages already observed that "joy is called by ten names." This is quite natural, for to the Jew the entire universe forms one happy symphony of joyousness in which even inanimate nature participates eagerly. To the Jew the Law is not an onerous burden. Therefore one must not serve the Lord with gloom and fear, but with joy and gladness. The appeal to rejoice is reiterated in virtually all books of the Bible. The Pentateuch demands: "Thou shalt rejoice in all the good which the Lord thy God hath given unto thee" (Deuteronomy 26:11). In the same vein Isaiah counsels: "Thou shalt rejoice in the Lord; thou shalt glory in the Holy One of Israel" (41:16), a call to joyousness that is reiterated over and over again, especially in the Psalms.

The Talmud asserts categorically that "there is no sadness before The Holy One, blessed be He" (Chagiga 5b). Consequently, one should not draw near to God out of sadness, but only with the joy that flows from the right performance of one's duties (Berachot 31a). This joy is the *simhah shel mitzvah*, the rejoicing in the commandment, a mood recommended by all teachers as the best disposition to be cultivated. One must be happy and joyous in the performance of one's duties and especially in the hour when one approaches God in prayer, for gloom is a barrier, as it were, to the knowledge of God.

One of the most beautiful tributes to the divine powers of joy comes from Yehudah Halevi, whose mystical-poetic soul was especially attuned to the creative potentialities of the pure, spiritual joy. In his *Kuzari* he explains that Judaism assigns equal importance to fear, love and joy in Divine service. "By each of them one can draw near to God. Yet, your sadness on a fast day does not please God more than your joy on the Sabbath and the holidays, provided it flows from a pious heart. . . . And if joy move you to sing and dance, it becomes worship and a bond of union between you and the Divine" (*Kuzari* II, 50).

Jews have a rare zest for making the most of the happy and joyous moments of life. They do not mix one joyous occasion with another, as for instance celebrating a marriage on a Sabbath or a holiday. Each joy is so important that a separate day must be assigned to it. Jews also have a special talent for glorifying the joyous occasion and draining its cup to the dregs. No matter how gloomy and fraught with sorrow the week may be, it ends with the Sabbath, a day that is all light, joy and delight; a day on which sorrow is as strictly interdicted as work. The Talmud relates that, before the Destruction of the Temple, the Festival of Water-drawing was the happiest and most joyous day in Israel. The Temple courts were gaily illuminated; there was dancing and singing and a torch procession in which the most eminent Sages participated. Joy ran high on that festival of thanksgiving for the blessing of the rain. The Talmud asserts that "he who has not witnessed the joy of the Festival of Water-drawing has never seen joy in his life." The pious Hillel would eagerly participate in the festivities, while such an eminent Sage as Rabbi Simeon ben Gamaliel would delight the festival assembly by exhibiting his virtuosity as a juggler of eight burning torches. In the ancient Orient nature festivals of this kind invariably were marked by wild orgies. But not so in Israel, for lest the exciting festive atmosphere—the light, the singing, the dancing—stir the senses of the men and women overmuch, the Sages decreed that on the Festival of Water-drawing men and women must be seated separately, which, incidentally, seems in no wise to have impaired the joyousness and innocent frolic.

Judaism recommends the spiritualized and intellectualized joy in all the good things of this earth. Even the "Divine Presence" does not dwell among the gloomy, but only with those who rejoice and, through their joy, affirm the goodness of life and the world.

The exaltation of the religious qualities of joy in Judaism goes hand in hand with a profound appreciation of beauty. How far Judaism is from any vestige of asceticism may be gauged from the fact that it praises beauty, even the physical charms of woman, as the handiwork of God and his gracious gift to mankind. To the Jew, beauty is not the lure of satan, as so many Christian saints propounded, but the work of God. Beauty is not sinful but the essence of goodness. According to the Rabbis, God led Adam about the Garden of Eden and pointed out to him all its lovely trees, saying "My beautiful and glorious works have all been created for your sake. Take heed, therefore, not to corrupt or destroy My world" (Kohelet Rabbah 7:13).

Man is the crown of creation, its very purpose, as it were. He should therefore enjoy all the beauty and goodness of creation, for abstinence and disdain of beauty are, according to the religious view of Judaism, sinful frustrations of the very purpose of the Creator.

One must, therefore, be alert to beauty; enjoy it and be moved by it to religious sentiments. Thus Rabbi Judah taught that when one sees the trees in bloom, he should say "Blessed be He in Whose world there is not missing a thing and Who has created beautiful creatures and beautiful trees to gladden the sons of men" (Berachot 43b). Even the fragrance of the flowers must not go unnoticed; the pious Jew is bidden to breathe his fill of its sweetness, and thank God for the blessing (Berachot 43b).

In contradistinction to Christianity, which regards poverty, celibacy and solitude as singularly conducive to piety, and disparages joy and beauty as sinful, Judaism affirms man's God-given right to the fullest permissible cup of this-worldly happiness in material blessings, in marriage, in a well integrated community life and in a keen and alert enjoyment and appreciation of the beauty and the perfection of creation. Although Judaism, together with Christianity, looks forward to a better world-to-come, it still does not disdain this world which is the handiwork of God. "The golden mean" of the sensible and measured acceptance and enjoyment of life and its blessings advocated by Judaism is therefore irreconcilable with the basic Christian attitude of asceticism which regards abstinence from life necessities as pious and pleasing to God.

CHAPTER VI

Faith vs. Law

THE LAWS OF THE TORAH are to Judaism the quintessence of permanent goodness. Christianity, on the other hand, advances its claims on the strength that the "Law" is superseded and abrogated by "Faith" in Jesus. From the New Testament to virtually the latest book on Christian theology the supposedly irreconcilable antagonism of "Law" and "Faith" has been zealously reiterated by Christian theologians throughout nineteen centuries. In countless learned dissertations generations upon generations of Christians have been propounding the inferiority of the "Law" in comparison with "Faith." Moreover, the "Law" and "Faith" have been placed into an incompatible juxtaposition, as if the one spelled the annihilation of the other and ritual observance implied eo ipso also the negation of faith.

The repudiation of the Law and the claim to possess not only a substitute but a superior successor to it has been the contention of Christianity since its inception. The "good news" of the Apostles was chiefly that the chains of the Law had been lifted and superseded by Faith in the love manifest in Jesus' ministry and sacrifice.

It is generally accepted by Jewish scholars also that Jesus believed in the eternal validity of the Torah and observed all its minutiae. In support of this view are cited his famous words: "Do not suppose that I have come to do away with the Law or the Prophets. I have not come to do away with them but to enforce them. For I tell you, as long as heaven and earth endure, not one dotting of an *i* or crossing of a *t* will be dropped from the Law until it is all observed. Anyone, therefore, who weakens one of the slightest of these commands, and teaches others to do so, will be ranked lowest in the Kingdom of Heaven; but anyone who observes them and teaches others to do so will be ranked high in the Kingdom of Heaven" (Matthew 5:17–19). Notwithstanding this affirmation of the eternal validity of the Law, however, Jesus himself laid the foundation for its abrogation by his followers. A few examples will illustrate this:

Once Jesus and his disciples walked on a Sabbath through the wheat fields. His companions were hungry and they picked and ate ears of wheat. When the Rabbis censured them for this breach of the Sabbath law, Jesus replied "the Son of Man is master of the Sabbath" (Matthew 12:1–8). Now, the Talmud, too, asserts that the Sabbath was given to man rather than man being surrendered to the Sabbath. In emergencies, where human life is at stake, the violation of the Sabbath rest is not only permitted but obligatory. In the case of Jesus' disciples' desecration of the Sabbath, however, no such emergency existed. And Jesus' recourse to the rabbinically sanctioned desecration of the Sabbath was therefore inappropriate and unlawful. Moreover, Jesus conveyed the impression that solely he, "the Son of Man," was master of the Sabbath, thus arrogating to himself a privilege which rabbinic Judaism democratically grants to every man and woman and child in a state necessitating the breaking of the Sabbath rest.

There is, however, even more conclusive evidence of Jesus'

negative attitude to the "Law." Thus, to the question concerning the qualifications for life eternal, he enumerated only six of the ten commandments (do not murder, do not commit adultery, do not steal, do not bear false witness, do not defraud, honor your father and your mother), omitting the four commandments of religious and ceremonial obligations, namely, belief in God, the prohibition of idolatry, the taking of the name of God in vain, and the commandment of the sanctification of the Sabbath (Mark 10:17–19).

Jesus' most outspoken rejection of the Law is presented by the parable of the old and the new that cannot be combined. "No one sews a new patch of unshrunken cloth on an old coat; or if he does, the patch tears away, the new from the old, and makes the hole worse than ever. And no one pours new wine into old wine-skins; or if he does, the wine bursts the skins. New wine has to be put into fresh skins" (Mark 2:21–22). This parable was offered in reply to the question why he and his disciples failed to keep a fast observed by the Pharisees (and consequently a legally binding fast as instituted by the teachers of the Law) and even by John the Baptist's disciples.

In Jesus' teachings opposition and hostility to the "Law" are merely adumbrated, although distinctly enough to provide Paul, the wizard of propaganda and organization who built the Church, with sufficient justification to declare the era of the "Law" at end and to proclaim the aeon of "Faith." The unpassable gulf between Judaism and Christianity appears widest in the New Testament passages recording Paul's bitter attacks against the Law. To Paul the Law was the most formidable enemy obstructing the dissemination and progress of "the good news." He therefore relentlessly disparaged the Law as worthless, obsolete and harmful, contrasting the "slavery" of those who live under the Law with "the freedom" of those who believe in Jesus (Galatians 2:4). Moreover, he disputed the justification of laws for any but criminals: "I agree that the Law is excellent—provided it is legitimately used, with the understanding that law is not intended for upright men but for the lawless and disorderly, the godless and irreligious, the irreverent and profane, men who kill their fathers or mothers, murderers, immoral people, men sexually perverted, kidnappers, liars, perjurers, or whatever else is contrary to sound teaching, as set forth in the glorious good news of the blessed God with which I have been entrusted" (I Timothy 1:8–11).

The idea that laws are only meant for sinners is irreconcilable with the traditional Jewish regard for the Law to whose authority even God Himself submits. The negation of the Law is the negation of Judaism. Paul, who had been trained in the schools of the Pharisees, was fully aware of this, and he therefore zealously attacked the Law, hoping that these assaults would lead to its downfall. Over and over again, Paul proclaimed that "Christ marks the termination of Law" (Romans 10:4), emphasizing that "by doing what the Law commands no one can be made upright" (Galatians 2:16).

The Christian doctrine of salvation rests on the belief in Jesus, who died on the cross to atone for the sins of mankind. This idea, of course, is contrary to the Jewish conviction that atonement and subsequent salvation are procured through repentance and faithful adherence to the Law. Christianity *had* to disown the Law, for, as Paul correctly saw, "if uprightness could be secured through the Law, then Christ died for nothing" (Galatians 2:21). In other words, Christianity rejects the Law since it represents the negation of the Christian claims. Paul understood this perfectly. It was therefore the pursuit of a definite strategy, rather than mere blind hatred, that was the propelling power of his interminable attacks upon the Law whose existence implies that "Christ died for nothing."

There is no compromise possible between the Law and

Faith as defined by Paul. None knew this better than Paul himself and so he tirelessly contrasted the "bondage" of men under the "Law" with the "freedom" of "Faith" that breaks and discards those chains. "For no human being can be made upright in the sight of God by observing the Law. All that the Law can do is to make man conscious of sin" (Romans 3:20). For "if it had not been for the Law, I should never have learned what sin was; I should not have known what it was to covet if the Law had not said, 'You must not covet.' That command gave sin an opening and led me to all sorts of covetous ways, for sin is lifeless without Law" (Romans 7:7–8).

Such tortuous argumentation led Paul to conclude that the Law was "a curse" from which there was only one escape: faith in Jesus. As Paul phrased it, "Christ ransomed us from the Law's curse by taking our curse upon himself" (Galatians 3:13).

THE IDEA that the Law had been superseded by faith gave rise in turn to the doctrine that "the true Israel" are not the Jews but the heathen who accept "the good news" of redemption through faith. To Paul "the real descendants of Abraham are the men of faith" (Galatians 3:7). In endless casuistries Paul and his successors demonstrated, by doing violence to the text of the Hebrew Bible, that the Divine promise to Abraham "did not come to him or his descendants through the Law, but through the uprightness that resulted from his faith" (Romans 4:13). Paul had to defend this position, just as he had to insist that Jesus' sacrificial death spelled the annihilation of the Law, "for," he continued in the dissertation on why Abraham's blessing rests on those who believe in Jesus, "if it is the adherents of the Law who are to possess it [the blessing], faith is nullified and the promise amounts to nothing" (Romans 4:14).

The Law is therefore Paul's most hated enemy. And not

merely because, as he charges, "the Law only brings down God's wrath; where there is no law, there is no violation of it" (Romans 4:15), but because he recognizes in the Law the eternal negation of the Christian claims and beliefs. The life of Christianity hinges, as it were, upon the nullification of the Law, even as the existence of Judaism is first and last predicated upon its preservation. Paul and his successors invariably chose the Law as the first aim of their attacks against Judaism. The realization that the Law renders Jesus' death futile and the faith in him empty, has been rankling in and poisoning the hearts of Christians through the ages. Even in our enlightened age Christian theologians persist in denouncing and deprecating the Law, for Christianity can only justify itself and demonstrate its worth by disproving and annihilating the Law.

Their respective attitudes to the Law cannot but divide Judaism and Christianity, especially since Paul's fanatical hatred and abuse of the Law and its representative teachers has had tragic repercussions. Even modern Christianity sees in the Law primarily a primitive instrument which makes men conscious of sin without affording them salvation. To Judaism, however, the Law is the royal road to faith and goodness; the Divine guidance which makes it possible for man to know and do the will of his Father in heaven. As a result of the Paulinian deprecation of the Law, Christians regard it as a sinister force of darkness and cheerlessness; a force of compulsion and slavery in contradistinction to "Christian freedom." To the Jews, however, the Law has always been the choicest blessing of a loving and merciful God.

The tributes and testimonies to the excellency of the soulful qualities of the Law, scattered throughout the Bible, the Talmud and Jewish religious literature of all centuries, amply prove that Jews have invariably sought and found soul satisfaction and an answer to all their religious-spiritual needs in the Torah, which is much more than legislation. Thanks to this all-sufficiency of the Torah, the Psalmist proclaimed: "The Law of the Lord is perfect, restoring the soul. . . ." (Psalms 19:8). The pious, therefore, finds "his delight in the Law of the Lord" (Psalms 1:2). Over and over again we find in the Psalms the terms of "delight" and "love" associated with the study and observance of the Law:

> I *delight* to do Thy will, O my God;
> Yea, Thy Law is in my inmost parts.
>   (Psalms 40:9)

> I *delight* in Thy Law. . . .
> The Law of Thy mouth is better unto me than thou-
>   sands of gold and silver.
>   (Psalms 119:70–72)

> Oh how I *love* Thy Law!
> It is my meditation all the day.
>   (Psalms 119:97)

> I *rejoice* at Thy word,
> As one that findeth great spoil.
> I hate and abhor falsehood;
> Thy Law do I *love*.

> Seven times a day do I praise Thee,
> Because of Thy righteous ordinances.

> Great peace have they that *love* Thy Law,
> And there is no stumbling for them.
>   (Psalms 119:162–165)

> Unless Thy Law had been my *delight*,
> I should have perished in my affliction.
>   (Psalms 119:92)

These passages not only prove that to the Jew "the commandment is a lamp and the Law a light" (Proverbs 6:23), but also that he finds in it the abundance of comfort and strength of faith.

IN ORDER TO APPRECIATE FULLY the Jewish love of the Torah, one must read the hundreds upon hundreds of Rabbinic passages glorifying it as the very essence of mercy, goodness, tenderness and consolation, precisely those qualities which Christianity denies from the Law and assigns to "Christian love." But the Torah is not only the symbol and medium of Divine love—it is also the example of and spur to perfection, the meaning of Jewish existence and the purpose of the world. There is no great and inspiring ideal, no blessing and no desirable state of perfection but has been identified or connected with the Law by the Jewish people. To them the Torah is "light" (Proverbs 6:23; Megillah 16b); it is the "glory of the sons of man" (Derech Eretz Zuta 75) and the vitalizing and energizing life sap, for, according to a talmudic opinion, "the dry bones" of which the Prophet Ezekiel (37:4) speaks are none other than "persons in whom there is not the sap of the commandment" (Sanhedrin 92b).

While Paul saw in the Law nothing else but a restraining and punitive force, Judaism regards it as the very foundation of the world and the instrument of the preservation of the universe. The Agadah, therefore, represents God as addressing himself to Israel: "If you study the Law, you render a good deed to My world. For if not for the Law, the world would return to the state of being desolate and waste" (Devarim Rabba; Nizzovim; VIII, 5). It is the pre-existent (Zebochim 116a) foundation of the world which can never pass out of existence.

But the awe and respect in which the Law is held does not

diminish the love Israel has for it, a love that makes the Torah appear as the most beautiful bride possessed of ravishing
charms and full of kindly tenderness. Thus the Torah is lik-
ened to the refreshing, life-restoring goodness of water, the
sweetness of honey and milk, the joy and strength contained
in wine, and the tender healing power of oil. It is an "elixir of
life" that brings healing to all men and affords protection
against all evils. It is a white-hot fire which, though it does
not consume its guardians, burns in eternal strength and
majesty.

There are many touching talmudic allegories symbolizing
Israel's love for the Law and the comfort and consolation
derived from it. It is their writ of Divine election, as it were;
God's promissory note that His pledges to the fathers will be
honored at the appointed time. Because of the Torah, Israel
does not despair. And so, at the end of the days, when God
will say to Israel: "My children, I am astonished you have
waited for me all these years," Israel will answer that this was
but natural as they had the Law. Of course, "if it had not been
for the Torah which Thou didst write for us, the nations long
ago would have estranged us from Thee" (Pesikta de'Rav
Kahana edited by Buber, c. XIX, p. 139b).

The Law and its minutiae are, therefore, to the Jew not a
burden, as the Christian interpreters of Judaism regard it, but
a glorious distinction. The words of Song of Songs, "Thou
art beautiful," meant to the Rabbis, rejoicing in the sweetness and the privilege of the possession of the Law, that Israel
is beautiful "through the commandments," which they happily enumerated. And it is significant that this enumeration
includes both "deeds of lovingkindness" and the laws of purely
ceremonial character (Shir Hashirim Rabbah 1:5), for Judaism has never recognized a distinction or differentiation between the laws commanding lovingkindness and the laws of
purely ceremonial significance. Both are of the woof and warp

of the Torah; both are interwoven in its pattern and cannot exist separately.

The perennial Christian objections to the Law as a force externalizing religion and obliterating "faith" are not based on facts. Judaism places the utmost emphasis on the practice of lovingkindness and the observance of the ceremonial law in the right spirit and with an undivided heart. For God "demands the heart" and not mere lip service. On the other hand, however, Judaism asserts that "the heart" and "emotion" are not sufficiently stable to guarantee justice, which must be removed from the realm of subjective feeling and be firmly established in the immutable, eternal and objective permanency of the Law. Judaism sees no antithesis between the Law and Faith for both are meant and destined to complement and supplement each other. The human being is a synthesis of body *and* soul, and analogously the Law and Faith are required to lead man to the ethical perfection for which he is destined. Thanks to this organic and natural union of the ceremonial aspects of religion with faith, Jewish Law has invariably been more than mere legislation. There has always been the awareness that the Law, in its entirety, is not the end but the means toward the ethicization of mankind and the enthronement of humane righteousness.

CHRISTIANITY'S CLAIM to be the rightful heir to the Prophetic religion of love, supposedly disowned by the "legalist" rabbis, is invalidated by incontrovertible facts. Judaism knows of no antagonism between the Prophets and the Rabbis. If the Prophets stressed neighborly love and justice and righteousness as the ideal of piety, so did the Rabbis; and if the Rabbis emphasized the importance of the sanctification of the Sabbath and the right worship of the Only God, so did the Prophets. There is no antithesis and no conflict between the teachings of the Prophets and those of the Rabbis, for, "since the day when the Temple was destroyed, prophecy has been taken from the Prophets and given to the Sages" (Bava Batra 12a). Both Prophets and Sages were devoted to the same religious ideals; they were guided by the same Law, which aims at the perfection of the physical and the spiritual aspects of life and therefore does not differentiate between "ceremonialism" and "ethics." In Judaism ceremonies are symbolical of ethics, and ethics is translated into reality by means of ceremonial observances.

As a result, Judaism can neither understand nor accept the Christian differentiation between "the head" and "the heart," or between the "Law" and "Faith," for they form one inseparable, organic whole in the Jewish scheme. For the purpose of the Law is "twofold: the well-being of the soul and the well-being of the body. The well-being of the soul is advanced by correct opinions communicated to the people according to their capacity. . . . The well-being of the body is established by the proper management of human relations. This can be achieved in two ways: first, by removing all violence from our midst, that is to say, that we refrain from doing as we please, desire and are able to do, but contribute, every one of us, toward the common good. Secondly, inculcating such good morals as must result in a perfect state. . . . The latter object is the primary need. It is also carefully and minutely dealt with in the Torah, for the well-being of the soul is predicated on that of the body. . . ." (Maimonides, *Guide of the Perplexed*, III, 27).

The Law is therefore not, as Christianity has been insisting since its inception, a curse but a blessing. In the words of Maimonides: "The ordinances of the Torah are not punishment for the world, but a medium of mercy, kindness and peace" (Hilchot Shabbat II, 3). And "love," which Christianity has claimed as its own peculiar gift to mankind, is the very medium and purpose of the Law, for "he who does the commandment because of love is superior to him who does it because of fear" (Sota 31b). Judaism glories those who, impelled by love, "rush eagerly toward the performance of the religious duties" (Pesachim 4a). Still, emotion cannot be entrusted with the full responsibility for human conduct. This Kantian conviction was at the root of the Sages' insistence on faithful compliance with the letter—but not at the expense of the spiritual values—of the Law. And so if Rabbi Hanina asserted that it is more meritorious to comply with the commandment than to do something equally or more praiseworthy that is not commanded (Kiddushin 31a), he did not intend to glorify the external shell of the Law but to impress upon his disciples the sacredness of duty, the inescapable moral obligation of the Law as the guide to moral perfection.

It would be erroneous to think that the ancient Rabbis—the "Pharisees" whom Jesus and Paul so bitterly and unjustly denounced—were not aware of the superfluity of the ceremonial Law from the viewpoint of God. They did not hesitate to assert that to God it does not matter one bit how we slaughter the animals or what we eat. They maintained, however, that these ceremonial laws were given as a discipline "to purify God's creatures" (Tanchuma, edited by Buber, Shemini 15b). The thought that the ceremonial law is an instrument of moral perfection recurs repeatedly in talmudic literature, providing conclusive proof that the Sages were far from being cold legalists but were keenly alert to the problems of ethics.

Judaism holds that ethics and morality are safeguarded and advanced by the Law; Christianity contends that they are stifled and frustrated by the Law. Today, as in the days of Paul and his attacks against the Law and its teachers, Christianity adheres to the view that the Law is a force or darkness in opposition to the new Christian light of faith and love. As a result, there is virtually no book in the multitude of volumes by Christian theologians treating of the problems of the Law which does not stress, in one form or another, sometimes with more restraint and sometimes with less, that there is an inherent contradiction between obedience to the Law and genuine religiousness, a point which Jews will never concede. For the reality of Jewish law and life conclusively proves this charge is wrong. Even modern, progressive and tolerant Christian scholars find it impossible to free themselves from this error. Thus, for instance, Professor Ernest F. Scott writes:

"Against the Judaism of his day Jesus repeatedly brings the charge that it led to formalism and hypocrisy; and we cannot doubt that the criticism was substantially just. Certainly it was never meant to include all who governed their lives by the Law, but it exposed one weakness which was inherent in the legal system. The attempt to enforce obedience by law had destroyed the very spring and motive of true obedience.

". . . the religion of the Law had its outcome in pride and self-righteousness. It was chiefly on this ground that Jesus condemned the scribes and the Pharisees, and Paul likewise dwells on this as the cardinal defect of the Law. These accusations have often been indignantly denied, but the truth of them appears self-evident. When it was assumed that the whole will of God was comprised in a number of stated rules, men could easily persuade themselves that they had obeyed it perfectly. . . . The effect of the Law, as Paul perceived, was to create an attitude of mind which was the precise opposite of the true religious temper.

"These, according to the New Testament, were the outstanding defects of Judaism, and it is useless to deny their reality" (*The Gospel and Its Tributaries*, 1928, pp. 39–40).

Although Professor Scott is ready to admit "that the New Testament account of the Law is biased by controversial aims and is sometimes unduly harsh," he yet holds that "on a deeper view we can perceive that it is not only valid, but lays bare, with marvellous penetration, the radical defects of the legal system" (*op. cit.*, p. 36).

As we are not concerned with apology, we need not dwell on the strange contradiction in this eminent New Testament scholar's summary, who characterizes the Christian estimate of the Law as "biased" and unduly "harsh" and yet raises the traditional charges of "the radical defects of the legal system." This quotation should prove how difficult and virtually impossible it is to reconcile the views of Judaism and Christianity on the role of the Law. The claims advanced on its behalf by the former are categorically denied by the latter, which moreover maintains that the Law has outlived its usefulness and has been superseded by the Christian substitute, "faith" in Jesus and the belief in his sacrificial death and resurrection.

To JUDAISM the Law is synonymous with eternity. Being the revealed will and the guidance of God to mankind (and not merely to Israel!), the Law can never be abrogated and superseded. Moreover, as the Law is informed by the wisdom and goodness of God, it is all perfect and complete and not in need of any addition or improvement. Even the interpretation of the Law, in accordance with the traditional hermeneutical rules, are imminent in its very body and character. The Sages therefore interpreted the Pentateuchal passage, "for this commandment. . . . is not in heaven" (Deuteronomy 30:11f) as a distinct warning to the Israelites. "Lest you say, another Moses is to arise and to bring us another Law from heaven, therefore, I make it known to you now that it is not in heaven, meaning nothing is left in heaven." There can be no new law to supersede the Law given by Moses, for as Rabbi Hanina taught: "The Law and all the implements by which it is carried out have been given, namely, modesty, benevolence, uprightness and reward" (Deuteronomy Rabba, Nitzavim, VIII, 6).

The eternal validity of the Torah is part of authoritative Jewish belief as defined by Maimonides. It is the ninth of the "Thirteen Articles of Belief" which the Jew proclaims in his daily prayers: "I believe with perfect faith that this Torah will never be changed and that the Creator, blessed be His name, will never give us another *Torah*." In the introduction to the Mishnah tractate *Chelek*, where the "Thirteen Articles of Faith" are listed in a fuller form than in the prayerbook, Maimonides avows the eternal validity of the Torah in the following manner: "This Torah of Moses will not be abrogated and no other Torah will come from God. Nothing is to be added to it nor taken away from it, neither in the written nor in the oral Law as it is said: 'Thou shalt not add thereto nor diminish from it'" (Deuteronomy 31:1).

Even still more explicitly this basic Jewish tenet is stated and elaborated in Maimonides' Code: "It is a distinct and explicitly stated feature of the Law that it is an ordinance to endure for all eternity, and it does not admit of any alteration, diminution or addition. . . . Hence we learn that no Prophet has permission to introduce any innovation at any future time. Should, therefore, a man arise, either from among the nations or from among Israel, and perform any sign or miracle and declare that God has sent him to add any commandments or to abrogate any commandment or to explain any of the commandments otherwise than we have heard from Moses; or should he declare that the commandments which have been ordained for the Israelites are not for all time and for all generations, but were only temporary enactments; behold, this man is indeed a false prophet, for he indeed comes to refute the prophecy of Moses" (Hilchot Yesodei Ha-Torah 9:1).

This, then, has been the Jewish attitude through the ages; a position which has been no less staunchly defended than the Christian claim that Jesus is the rightful abrogator of the Law. Were Judaism to concede the legitimacy of the Christian charges against the Law it would thereby sign its death warrant, just as Christianity, by recognizing the validity of the Law, would acknowledge that, as Paul phrased it, "Christ died for nothing" (Galatians 2:21). The Law, therefore, will forever be the strongest element of contention between Judaism and Christianity, for its existence spells the negation of Christianity and its abrogation the negation of Judaism.

There is no patent solution for this conflict, except the type of tolerance Judaism and its best minds have shown to the members of other religions, a tolerance which is well epitomized in the talmudic statement that if the Jews are rendered meritorious through the medium of the Law, the non-Jews, together with the Jews, can acquire merit in the sight of God through deeds of lovingkindness.

CHAPTER VII

The Interpretation of Judaism

Our presentation of the differences between Judaism and Christianity would be incomplete without an examination of the profound dissimilarities in Judaism's self-appraisal of its role and destiny and Christianity's judgment on these. While Judaism maintains that its Divine mission and the Divine promises pledged to its "founding fathers" are in no way affected or rendered obsolete by the emergence of Christianity on the stage of history, the latter has consistently proclaimed, from its very birth, that its entrance into the world marked the end of the Jewish dispensation and that all the promises given to the Jews will henceforth apply to Christians only.

It is this attitude, more than anything else, which has divided, and is dividing, the two faiths. The claim, first advanced by Paul, that the confessors of Christianity are "the true Israel of God" (Galatians 6:16), implies the rejection of the Jews, is one of those basic Christian beliefs which has been vigorously opposed by the Synagogue, for any compromise with it would be tantamount to the signing of her own death verdict.

Christianity was from the very first a "protest religion" which militantly opposed the faith from which it had sprung. As all "protest movements" it sought to prove its own worth by negating the worth and validity of the religion from which it derived virtually its entire equipment. The denial of the validity of the Jewish message and mission thus became the chief task of the Apostles and of Christian spokesmen to this very day. It is a strange phenomenon that while Jewish religious teachers and thinkers, even in the darkest eras of persecution at the hands of the Church, took pains to stress that Christianity is one of the paths that, by weaning the heathen from idolatry, will eventually lead to the right knowledge of God, Christian teachers and theologians, from Paul's days to the present time, have written entire libraries with no other aim but to prove the eternal "rejection" and perdition of Judaism and its confessors.

The classical Christian interpretation of Judaism labels it as "the religion of death" (II Corinthians 3:6), maintaining that its confessors "for their want of faith were broken off" (Romans 11:20). Moreover, Paul, by a daring piece of exegesis, "proved" that the Jews are the descendants of Abraham's son by Hagar, the slave girl, while those who believe in Jesus are the true descendants of Isaac and the recipients of the blessings promised to him (Galatians 4:22–31). In other words, not the Jews but the confessors of Christianity are the people of the Divine covenant and "chosen." Professor Conrad Moehlman, one of the foremost liberal Protestant theologians of our time, summarizes the traditional Christian interpretation of Judaism (to which he, however, does not assent) as follows:

During the four centuries of silence between the close of the Old Testament period proper about the time of Malachi and the beginning of the Christian period, the Jews became blind to prophecy and changed the divine law into the legalism of the scribes. *Israel was the covenant people to the end of the Old Testament period.* Israel did not lose the covenant in the days of Abraham or the epoch of Moses but only four centuries before Christ. Thus the entire Old Testament was of God, inspired in every jot and tittle, and could be taken over in its entirety by Christianity.

Jesus of Nazareth continued the Old Testament prophets. The Jewish people originally had the prerogative but when Israel cast off its messiah, God cast it off. Since God has decided the issue, the Christian must accept the verdict of God and treat the Jew accordingly. The rights and privileges of the Jew under the Old Covenant have been transferred to the Gentile Christians (*The Christian-Jewish Tragedy*, pp. 209f).

Judaism was thus adjudged as "rejected" and so it became feasible to enthrone Christianity as the religion of "chosenness." The authoritative Christian view on the "rejection" of the Jews and Christianity's entrance upon their heritage was epitomized as follows by the late Professor Von Harnack:

The chosen people throughout was the Christian people, which always existed in a sort of latent condition though it only came to light at first with Christ. From the outset the Jewish people had lost the promise; indeed, it was a question whether it had ever been meant for them at all. In any case, the literal interpretation of God's revealed will proved that the people had been forsaken by God and had fallen under the sway of the devil. As this was quite clear, the final step had now to be taken, the final sentence had now to be pronounced; *the Old Testament, from cover to cover, has nothing whatsoever to do with the Jews.* Illegally and insolently, the Jews had seized upon it, they had confiscated it, and tried to claim it as their own property. They had falsified it by their exposition and even by correction and omission. It would be a sin for Christians to say 'The Book belongs to us and the Jews.' No; the Book belongs, now and evermore, to none but Christians! (Adolph Von Harnack: *Mission and Expansion*, I p. 34, 65ff—quoted by Moehlman, *op. cit.*, pp. 206f).

Professor Von Harnack was fair enough to admit that "such an injustice as that done by the Gentile church to Judaism is almost unprecedented in the annals of history. The Gentile church stripped it of everything, she took away its sacred book; herself a transformation of Judaism, she cut off all connection with the parent religion. The daughter first robbed her mother and then repudiated her" (*Mission and Expansion,* I p. 69—quoted by Moehlman, *op. cit.*, p. 211).

It is significant that the enmity toward Judaism and the denial of its truth is not a late development but was already very pronounced in the New Testament era. Paul's Epistles emphasize insistently that the "natural Israel" of the Synagogue has been supplanted, in all respects, by the "true Israel" of the Church.

VARIOUS religious bodies in this country of late have been engaged in purging from their textbooks passages that deprecate other faiths and thus may easily foster prejudice and intolerance. Such endeavors are to be encouraged for they augur a better understanding and kindlier relations between the different faiths. It remains doubtful, however, of what avail the purging of Christian textbooks can be as long as the New Testament, sacred to all of Christianity, is a virtual armory of anti-Jewish statements and utterances. Of what avail are "good will" efforts and profuse acknowledgments of the Jews' innocence of Jesus' death by well-meaning Christians when the New Testament lays the guilt for Jesus' death at the door of the Jews? As the New Testament is the Bible of *all* Christians, it is logical to conclude that as long as the New Testament will retain its place in Christian worship and study there will be little use in emphasizing that the Jews did not kill Jesus . . . There is an irreconcilable discrepancy between "good will" efforts and the portrait of the Jews painted by the Gospels. Of what avail are all the charitable and kind acknowledgments of the religious values of Judaism by progressive Christian theologians when the Christian Bible emphasizes that the Jews and their faith are rejected for all eternity?

The New Testament represents Judaism as a stunted, backward and obsolete religion without "fulfilment" and lacking "truth." Consequently it has no longer any place in the world. There are few books on the Bible or theology by Christian authors which refrain from stressing the supposed antagonism of "Old Testament legalism" and "New Testament faith grounded in love." The general Christian attitude to the "Old Testament," in vogue among liberal theologians as well, may be judged from this quotation from a volume *Liberal Theology* (Essays in honor of E. W. Lyman, 1942) where Professor Julius A. Bewer introduces his study on "Liberalism in the Old Testament" as follows:

> The particularism and nationalism with its exclusiveness, intolerance and hatred of foreign nations; the institutionalism with its externalism; and the legalism with its narrowness are so conspicious in the Old Testament, together with the crudities and cruelties of thought and practice, that the attempt to trace 'liberalism' in it may seem strange (*op. cit.*, p. 58).

The "dogma" of Jewish particularism is so deeply ingrained in the Christian mind that even scholars of repute cannot but imagine that any humanitarian stirring in Ancient Israel was the result of outside influence. Thus Dr. Bewer writes: "One hails with joy the few isolated liberal prophetic messages in Isaiah 19:23–24 and the Book of Jonah, the universal sweep of the apocalyptic hope in Isaiah 25:6–8 and in the eschatological psalms which anticipate the coming of God's Kingdom on earth . . . But even these are not altogether free from Jewish elements (except perhaps the Book of Jonah). Moreover, all this is not for the present but only for the future. For the present none seems to be thinking that all the nations are God's children. Or may we again except the Book of Jonah?

"Most likely this book came from the Hellenistic period when the Jews were in touch with Greek philosophy and civilization after they had been strongly influenced by the Persians during their rule" (*op. cit.*, pp. 67f).

It seems strange that a scholar of Professor Bewer's standing is unaware of the existence of scores upon scores of *Jewish* Bible passages proclaiming the universal sway of God's might and His loving concern for all mankind.

IN THE COURSE of the preparation of this volume, the present writer has examined a very large number of books on Christian theology, representing various denominations and shades of opinion. Although the authors consulted differ considerably in their interpretations of virtually all aspects of Christian belief and its history, there is remarkable unanimity on the interpretation of Judaism. Here the "orthodox" and the "liberals" meet on the common ground of the New Testament thesis of the rejection of Judaism. The "liberal" view may be characterized by this picturesque comment on Sargent's paintings of the "Synagogue" and the "Church" in a volume of *New Testament Studies* (edited by Edwin P. Booth, 1942). Writing on *Jesus and the Pharisees*, Professor Earl B. Marlatt acknowledges that the traditional Christian judgment of the Pharisees is untenable in the light of modern scholarship. This concession, however, does not influence his adherence to the traditional Christian interpretation of Judaism, as may be seen from the following:

> In the Corridor of the Prophets of the Boston Public Library is a powerful wall painting depicting John Singer Sargent's idea of 'The Synagogue.' Done in pastel shades, it presents an Amazonian figure, hoodwinked—tottering crown on her head, a broken scepter in her hand—clinging feverishly to draperies embroidered with apocalyptic fancies . . . Also in the Corridor of the Prophets is another painting representing Sargent's conception of 'The Church,' a maiden, clear-eyed and open-seeing, leaning upon a Personality, the crucified Christ, and holding in her hands a cup and a censer from which rise the symbols of facts—the Gospels of Mark, Matthew, Luke, and John. The picture is drenched with 'the light that never was on sea or land'; and yet the pedestal, supporting the Great White Throne and the Savior's swollen feet, is white like sepulchers. For eyes that see and minds that understand, it symbolizes the dust of 'dead men's bones' (*op. cit.*, p. 278 and p. 280).

"Hoodwinked—tottering crown—broken scepter—dead men's bones"—can Judaism assent to this characterization of its essence and its being?

After this presentation of a *liberal* Christian view, it will not be out of place if we cite also a *moderate orthodox* Christian estimate of Judaism and the Jews, as provided in *God in History*, a book by Professor Otto Piper of Princeton Theological Seminary. Writes Professor Piper:

> The loss of the Holy Land was the divine sign that Israel's universal mission had come to close . . . Israel's historical mis-

sion has been handed over to the fellowship which Christ gathered around him. The purpose of God in history is now carried out by the Church (*op. cit.*, p. 92).

Jews and Christians agree in their interpretation of Jewish history as far as the pre-Christian era is concerned: it was holy history. But their views differ when they turn to the destruction of Jerusalem in 70 A.D. and to the subsequent dispersion of the Jews. From the Christian point of view there is direct causal connection between these events and the crucifixion of Jesus. The fate of the Jews is the divine punishment for their rejection of the promised Messiah. The Jews, however, find fault with everyone except themselves. It is true that in our days some of them admit that it was a mistake or even a crime on the part of the Sanhedrin to sentence Christ to death. But personally they are not willing to share the responsibility for this atrocious crime.

Yet the death of Christ was not an isolated event in the history of His time, it was the logical and inevitable outcome of the attitude which Israel, as such, took towards the will of God. They distorted the Law and the Prophets, because they regarded their political and religious history as important in itself and thus they detracted from the divine purpose in history. Because of the way in which they interpreted their position they thought they could determine God's future revelations in advance. Thus they made themselves incapable of believing God, when in Jesus Christ He revealed His will in an entirely new and unexpected manner. Others were entirely negligent about the condition which God had attached to His covenant. They trusted in the fact that they were Abraham's seed and hoped for the 'luck of Jacob.' The result was shameless arrogance and moral and religious indifference. A conflict between these 'guardians' of Israel's tradition and Jesus was bound to be deadly. For, from the point of view of official Judaism, Jesus undermined the Law and questioned the divine mission of the chosen people. But His crucifixion was not the work of some Jewish rulers only, who in their injustice and envy hated Christ as their rival. For the rest of Israel—with the exception of the few who became Christians—followed their official leaders, and thereby tacitly approved of Jesus' pitiful end. Hence all Jews were responsible for His death. This is the reason they all have to endure the Divine punishment (*op. cit.*, pp. 90f).

The aim of this series of essays is not apologetic but descriptive. We are not concerned here with disproving Christian claims and charges but solely with the delineation of the differences between Judaism and Christianity. Our quoting excerpts of the type of Dr. Piper's estimate of Judaism and the Jews is motivated by no other intention than to illustrate the various shades of Christian opinion of Judaism. Dr. Piper's academic position warrants, however, the conclusion that his views are not mere personal opinions but authoritative utterances by a theologian and scholar who occupies a position of leadership in his Church. Perhaps Dr. Piper's views are presented with less restraint than has become customary among Christian theologians of late. But, in the final analysis, he only states the official view of the Churches that justifies their claims to be in possession of the truth with the charge of Judaism's rejection.

The Christian dogma of the "chosenness" of the Church, in place of the "chosen people" of the "Old Covenant," is central in Christianity. In fact, without this dogma Christianity would be unable to "prove" the legitimacy of its claims. For Christianity has raised itself to power, and maintained itself in power, by consistently asserting that it is "the true Israel of God" and that "the natural Israel" has been superseded and forced down from its erstwhile position.

Judaism maintains that the "Covenant with the fathers"

and the Torah have eternal validity and that "the true Israel of God" are those, and those alone, who confess the Unity of God as taught by the Torah, the sacred and eternally valid Divine teaching and message to Israel and mankind.

The fact that Judaism has survived for almost two thousand years the attacks of Christianity and has built an imposing structure of a diversified religious culture and civilization upon the foundation of the supposedly dead letter of the Law is sufficient proof that the Synagogue is a far cry from the "hoodwinked" figure—"tottering crown on her head, a broken scepter in her hand"—Christians depict her to be.

For Christianity to admit that the Old Covenant is still in force would be tantamount to signing its death warrant, just as it would spell the doom and end of Judaism were Jews to acknowledge the "New Dispensation." There is no way of bridging this gulf, except by the kind of tolerance Jewish teachers manifest in acknowledging Christianity, the daughter of Judaism, as it were, despite its youthful rebelliousness and immaturity, as a definite progress and advance over the idolatrous cults which it supplanted.

ANOTHER SIGNIFICANT element dividing Judaism and Christianity is presented by the Christian interpretation of the Old Testament.

To Judaism the Hebrew Bible (termed by Christians the "Old Testament") is first and last the revelation of God's will and His workings in Israel's destiny and how, in the future-to-come, He will through Israel, His "servant," make known and acceptable this will for righteousness and justice to all of mankind.

To Christianity the Old Testament has no intrinsic value besides being the preparation for the New Testament. This view, which in point of fact denies Judaism's right to life once the New Testament and the New Covenant were given, is utterly irreconcilable with the Jewish belief in the eternal validity of God's covenant with the people of Israel, the descendants in the flesh *and* in the spirit of Abraham.

The Christian doctrine of the New Covenant inevitably relegated the Old Testament to a place of secondary importance. The Church adopted the Hebrew Bible for no other reason than that it regarded it as a book of prophecies foretelling Jesus' career. Entire libraries have been written to prove "Christian fulfilments" foreshadowed in the Hebrew Bible.

Early Christianity, in order to be able to compete with Judaism, had of necessity to furnish evidence that it, too, was based upon authentic revelation. To be sure, the early Christians could point to Jesus as the symbol of this revelation and investiture with a religious mission. On the other hand, however, this was not enough in the tradition-minded Orient where claims to authority must be authenticated with ancestor proof. Early Christianity acquired that justification by the bold claim that all of the messianic predictions of the Hebrew Bible referred to none other than Jesus. The Old Testament thus became, first and last, the prediction of the New Testament, the deed and title, as it were, to the Christian claims of the messiahship of Jesus, in whom were supposedly fulfilled all the messianic promises of the Hebrew prophets. Accordingly, in the words of a distinguished Christian Bible scholar, "the life of Christ, the doctrines of the new dispensation, the fortunes of the Church would stand out clearly to the Christian eye on the pages of Scripture; the old congregation of Israel was felt to be a preparation for and a prediction of the new congregation of Christ; the chief interest for the Christian lay in the discovery of references to the gospel times, and in a thousand Old Testament passages he might find prophecies and illustrations of what was going on around him" (Crawford H. Toy, *Judaism and Christianity*, p. 137).

While the Churches insist, of course, on the immutable authenticity of this interpretation of the Old Testament, without which Christianity were bound to collapse, modern Protestant Bible critics, who no longer feel themselves bound by the accepted dogmas, are ready to grant that the traditional Christian interpretation of the Old Testament is without any justification whatsoever and controverted, moreover, by irrefutable evidence. Professor Moehlman candidly admits that "the perversion of the original meaning of Old Testament passages by the employment of allegory has been a continuous Christian affliction. This disease has ever been epidemic in Christianity, and no cure is known. It exists in countless forms according to the whim of its employer. Those suffering from it become thoroughly dishonest interpreters of the Old Testament without knowing it. As nothing can be done about it, the historian retains his sanity only by taking strong doses of common sense and humor" (*The Christian-Jewish Tragedy*, pp. 141f).

OSTENSIBLY, were the Churches ready to admit the baselessness of the Christian interpretation of the Old Testament, there would be no basic difference between their and our interpretation of Scripture. However this is not at all the case. Views like those propounded by Professor Moehlman are judged as heretical not only by Catholics and Protestant Fundamentalists but even by some liberal Protestant Churches. This, of course, does not imply that Christian Bible scholars are not aware of the unscientific character of the traditional Christian interpretation of the Old Testament. These difficulties, however, are often settled by the appeal of "faith" which justifies everything and resolves all contradictions. Thus, for instance, Cardinal Newman candidly admits that "a reader who came to the inspired text by himself, beyond the influence of that traditional acceptation which happily encompasses it, would be surprised to be told that the prophet's words, 'a virgin shall conceive, etc.' or 'let all the angels of God worship him,' refer to our Lord." What matters to the Cardinal is not the true meaning of the Hebrew text but the interpretation, no matter how fantastic, which is most conducive to the religious Christian purpose. And so he continues: "We readily submit our reason on competent authority, and accept certain events as an accomplishment of prediction which seems very far removed from them . . . Nor do we find a difficulty when St. Paul appeals to a text of the Old Testament which stands otherwise in our Hebrew copies . . . We receive such difficulties on faith and leave them to take care of themselves. Much less do we consider mere fulness in the interpretation, or definiteness, or again strangeness, as a sufficient reason for depriving the text, or the action to which it is applied, of the advantage of such interpretation. We make it no objection that the words themselves come short of it, or that the sacred writer did not contemplate it, or that a previous fulfilment satisfies it" (Cardinal Newman, *The Development of Christian Doctrine*, p. 103). There is no attempt on the part of Cardinal Newman to deny that the Apostles may have read into and derived from the Hebrew Bible things for which the text offers no basis whatsoever . . . But this matters little to the Christian believer for whom these interpretations are justified by faith in the authority of the Apostles and who therefore, despite incontrovertible evidence, insists on the interpretation of the Old Testament as a proof text for the New Testament.

It would be erroneous to assume that only Catholics hold such views. Except for a small minority of critical scholars, exemplified by Professor Moehlman, Protestant theologians and laymen alike hold fast to the traditional Christian interpretation of the Old Testament.

The view, however, that the New Testament is a superior fulfilment of the Old Testament is sounded by virtually all Christian Bible scholars. It is significant that even a scholar of the undisputed objectivity of Professor W. F. Albright feels constrained to prove, with quite a bit of straining of the standards of scholarship, the superiority, at least, of the New Testament and to imply that it is the fulfilment of the Old Testament. Thus, in discussing the Christian interpretation of suffering, Professor Albright writes: "Through Jesus' exaltation of suffering the old problem of the theodicy received a powerful new solution, one which had been at best only adumbrated in the Old Testament . . ." (*From the Stone Age to Christianity*, p. 302). In other words, Professor Albright, too, believes, although he says so only in veiled language, in the consummation of Hebraic thought and ethics in Christianity.

It is even more amazing, however, that this eminent Bible scholar and critic, finds it possible to adhere to the belief in Jesus' messianic mission and, consequently, in the fulfilment of the Hebrew messianic promises in him. For "the historian must recognize the presence of an important factual element in the Christian adoption of the Messianic tradition" (*op. cit.*, p. 308). Furthermore, "the historian cannot control the details of Jesus' birth and resurrection and thus has no right to pass judgment on their historicity" (*op. cit.*, p. 307). In other words, the central theme of the New Testament is beyond the grasp and reach of the critic.

To be sure, Professor Albright admits that there can be no absolute factual judgment. He therefore leaves the matter in the lap of the individual believer and to the Church "who are historically warranted in accepting the whole of the messianic framework of the Gospels or in regarding it as partly true literally and as partly true spiritually" (*op. cit.*, p. 308)—but, at any rate, there is no open disavowal of the traditional and unwarranted Christian interpretation of the Old Testament.

We have brought these quotations not to disprove Christianity but to strengthen our contention that the Hebrew Bible has an altogether different meaning for Christians, even for such an enlightened and progressive critic as Professor Albright, than for Jews.

For the sake of clarifying what is meant by New Testament interpretations of Old Testament passages which are inacceptable to Judaism we shall now present a few examples. First of all, there is a large number of Old Testament passages which, contrary to their true meanings, are interpreted as prophetic announcements of Jesus' ministry. Thus the Divine promise to Abraham, "in thee shall all the families of the earth be blessed" (Genesis 12:3; 18:18) is applied to the followers of Jesus: "So you see, the real descendants of Abraham are the men of faith. The Scripture foresaw that God would accept the heathen as upright in consequence of their faith, and preached the good news in advance to Abraham in the words, 'All the heathen will be blessed through you'" (Galatians 3:7ff).

When Moses, at the threshold of death, gave the Israelites a final summary of the Law, he also promised them, according to the Pentateuch, that "The Lord Thy God will raise up a prophet unto thee, from the midst of thee, of thy brethren, like unto me; unto him ye shall hearken" (Deuteronomy 18:15). According to Jewish interpretation, this passage refers to the Hebrew prophets; according to Christian teaching, however, this prophet is Jesus (see Acts, 3:22ff).

According to the Pentateuchal law a court of justice cannot convict a defendant on the testimony of one witness, but "at the mouth of two witnesses, or at the mouth of three witnesses, shall a matter be established" (Deuteronomy 19:15). Ostensibly, there is no "hidden meaning" to this unequivocal statement of a juridical principle. Nevertheless, this passage, too, is adduced as proof of Jesus' divine mission. He is represented as challenging the Pharisees as follows: "Why, in your own Law it is stated that the testimony of two persons is valid. Here I am testifying to myself, and the Father who has sent me testifies to me" (John 8:17).

The texts of the Hebrew Prophets, and especially that of Isaiah, provided the most fertile soil for Christian attempts of adducing proof for the truth of the New Testament. Thus Isaiah's vision of God's anger with recalcitrant Israel and of its punishment consisting in its ultimate inability to repent (Isaiah 6:9f), was interpreted by the Gospel writers as a clear prediction of the Jews' refusal to acknowledge and recognize Jesus. In other words, Isaiah chided his contemporaries in advance for the "sin" of not acknowledging Jesus some seven centuries later . . . (see Matthew 13:14f, compare Mark 4:12; Luke 8:10).

In his vision of the blessings of the Messianic age Isaiah promised the afflicted daughter of Israel: "And all thy children shall be taught of the Lord . . . " (Isaiah 54:13). Jesus applied that prophecy to himself: "In the prophets it is written, 'And all men will be taught by God.' Everyone who listens to the Father and learns from Him will come to me" (John 6:45). Professor Toy comments as follows on this passage and its New Testament reinterpretation: "The prophet, describing the ideal Israel of the future, represents all its members as entering into such personal relations with God that they shall need no human teacher. Jesus, adopting the words, applies them to the kingdom of God that he proclaimed; to him, as the sent of God, would come all those whom the Father had taught" (Toy, *Quotations in the New Testament*, p. 84). This interpretation lacks not only a basis in the Hebrew text but is, moreover, irreconcilable with the Jewish opposition to religious mediation.

Isaiah, the great consoler, encourages the afflicted Jews: "The spirit of the Lord God is upon me. Because the Lord hath anointed me to bring good tidings unto the humble, he hath sent me to bind up the brokenhearted, to proclaim liberty to the captives, and the opening of the eyes to them that are bound" (Isaiah 61:1f). The Gospels interpret this passage as referring to Jesus' ministry: "And when he came to Nazareth, where he had been brought up, and on the Sabbath he went to the synagogue, as he was accustomed to do, and stood up to read the Scriptures. And the roll of the prophet Isaiah was handed to him, and he unrolled it and found the place where it says . . . (here are quoted Isaiah 61:1f). And he rolled up the roll and gave it back to the attendant and sat down . . . And he began by saying to them: 'This passage of Scripture has been fulfilled here in your hearing today'" (Luke 4:18ff).

The eighth Psalm glorifies God: "Out of the mouth of babes and sucklings hast Thou founded strength" (Psalms 8:3). Jesus refers to this passage implying that the Psalmist predicted that he (Jesus) would be persecuted by the elders and acclaimed by the children (Matthew 21:16).

Another Psalm (78), glorying in the memory of God's love for Israel in the desert when "He caused manna to rain upon them for food, and gave them the corn of heaven" (Psalms 78:24), was likewise interpreted as foreshadowing Jesus' mission. "Jesus said to them: 'I tell you, Moses did not give you that bread out of heaven, but my Father gives you the bread out of heaven. . . .' Then they said to him, 'Give us that bread always, Master!' Jesus said to them, 'I am the bread that gives life . . .'" (John 6:32f).

Professor Toy remarks on Jesus' reply: "His answer is that God (not Moses) did indeed once give this bodily food from heaven to his people; but the true food of God is He (namely Jesus) whom God has appointed to be the spiritual life of the world" (Toy, *Quotations in the New Testament*, p. 83).

The Psalms are made to yield also evidence for Jesus' divine sonship. Thus the passage, "Thou art My son, this day I have begotten thee" (Psalms 2:7), which clearly refers to Israel, is claimed by Paul to be an announcement of the coming of the Son of God (see Letter to the Hebrews 1:5). Equally unsound and artificial is the application of Hosea's beautiful passage, "When Israel was a child, then I loved him, and out of Egypt I called My son . . ." (Hosea 11:1), to Jesus' parents' flight to Egypt to save their baby son from the wrath of Herod (Matthew 2:15). Jesus' return from Egypt was to the apostles a literal fulfilment of Hosea's words, "And out of Egypt I called My son . . . ."

IN A CLASS BY THEMSELVES are the many "New Testament" appropriations of the Hebrew messianic promises. The Gospel writers took over the Hebrew messianic doctrine in its entirety, and then reinterpreted it to fit Jesus and his precursor, John the Baptist. In this manner the most lucid and unequivocal prophetic promises for Israel's future restoration, with the coming of the Messiah, were forced into the procrustean bed of the Christian scheme of salvation. Thus, for instance, Isaiah's poetic vision,

> Hark! one calleth:
> Clear ye in the wilderness the way of the Lord,
> Make plain in the desert a highway for our God.
> Every valley shall be lifted up,
> And every mountain and hill shall be made low;
> And the rugged shall be made level,
> And the rough places a plain;
> And the glory of the Lord shall be revealed,
> And all flesh shall see it together;
> For the mouth of the Lord hath spoken it!
> (Isaiah 40:3–5)

was to the Gospels a prophecy referring to John the Baptist, who prepared the way for Jesus (Matthew 3:3; Mark 1:3; Luke 3:4–6; John 1:23).

To Christianity Jesus is not only the Son of God but also the Messiah on whose advent the hopes of all the Hebrew prophets were focused. However, in order to prove that Jesus was indeed *the* Messiah, the Gospel writers were faced with the task of demonstrating that his career, even in the most trivial details, was foretold by the prophets. As a result, numerous passages of the Hebrew Bible are quoted and interpreted in the Gospels in a sense diametrically opposed to the meaning with which tradition invested these passages. Thus such passages as, "The people that walked in darkness have seen a great light . . ." (Isaiah 9:1), and "Behold My servant, whom I uphold, Mine elect in whom My soul delighteth" (Isaiah 42:1ff) are to the Gospels and all believing Christians clear and distinct announcements of Jesus, although there is not a shred of doubt that the Hebrew prophet thought only of the *traditional* Jewish Messiah as the "great light" and "the servant whom My soul upholdeth." While Isaiah, especially his fifty-third chapter of the "Suffering Servant," has yielded the richest crop of "proofs" for Jesus, the other prophetic books, too, have been amply drawn upon.

Micah's prophecy that Bethlehem, the birthplace of King David, shall be again the cradle of a ruler of Israel (Micah 5:1) is utilized as follows:

"So he [King Herod] called together all the high priests and scribes of the people and asked them where the Christ was to be born. They said, 'At Bethlehem in Judah, for this is what the prophet wrote: And you, Bethlehem in Judah's land, you are by no means least important among the leading places of Judah, for from you will come a leader who will be the shepherd of my people Israel'" (Matthew 2:6).

In the same manner Zechariah's vision of the Messiah is taken as a proof for Jesus. The text, "Rejoice greatly, O daughter of Zion, shout, O daughter of Jerusalem; behold, thy king cometh unto thee. He is triumphant and victorious, lowly, and riding upon an ass, even upon a colt of the foal of an ass" (Zechariah 9:9) is interpreted in the Gospels as follows:

"Jesus sent two disciples on ahead, saying to them, 'Go to the village that lies in front, and you will at once find an ass tied there, and a colt with her. Untie her and bring them to me. If anyone says anything to you, you are to say 'The Master needs them; then he will send them at once.' Now this happened in fulfilment of what was said by the prophet . . ." (Matthew 21:5; John 12:14f).

Numerous proof texts also are taken from the Psalms. Thus the Psalmist's bitter complaint about the rebelliousness of the nations against God and His anointed, "Why are the nations in uproar? And why do the peoples mutter in vain? The kings of the earth stand up, and the rulers take counsel together, against the Lord, and against His anointed" (Psalm 2:1f) is quoted as referring to the plot against Jesus (Acts 4:25f). With the same ease the Gospels appropriate the passages, "The stone which the builders rejected is become the chief corner-stone. This is the Lord's doing; it is marvelous in our eyes" (Psalms 118:22f), as a clear prophecy of Jesus' rejection by the Jews (see Matthew 21:42; Mark 12:10f; a. o.).

The claims of Jesus' Davidic descent and birth by a virgin served as special incentives for searching the Hebrew Bible for "proofs." How flimsy the evidence for Jesus' connection with the House of David was considered, even by his contemporaries, may be seen from a passage in "John," which records that the people were perplexed how to reconcile the tradition of his Galilean origin (for which also numerous proof-texts are adduced) with the messianic promises. And so they queried: "What! Is the Messiah to come from Galilee? Do not the Scriptures say that the Messiah is to spring from the descendants of David and to come from the village of Bethlehem where David lived?" (John 7:42).

The dogma of the "Virgin Birth," which is based on Isaiah's prophecy, "Behold, *the young woman* shall conceive and shall bear a son and shall call his name Immanuel" (Isaiah 7:14), is probably the most widely discussed "New Testament" interpretation of a Hebrew text, contrary to the literal and accepted meaning. The reference to this passage in the annunciation of Jesus' birth (Matthew 1:18ff) is in fact based on the faulty translation of the Hebrew word *almah*, meaning "young woman," and rendered in the Greek Bible version with *partenos*—"virgin." Although all serious Christian Bible scholars admit that the Isaiah passage does not speak of a "virgin" but of a "young woman," the churches hold fast to the dogma of the "Virgin Birth." Commenting on the Isaiah passage and the circumstances that led to its misinterpretation, Louis D. Wallis, a Christian Bible scholar, writes:

"But when the New Testament finally emerged in its official form, it included a great deal of material whose purpose was to find in Hebrew history a series of mechanically 'inspired' predictions pointing to Jesus. This feature of the New Testament originated in the struggle which had been going on to explain the relation between Israel and the Christian Churches; and it was expressed in the reiterated formula 'that it might be fulfilled what was spoken by,' and so forth. New Testament pragmatism, accordingly, is responsible for dislocating the Hebrew prophets from their actual character as champions of justice and metamorphosing them into mechanically inspired foretellers, thus giving prophecy the character of mere unintelligent prediction . . .

"An instructive example of such manipulations is found in the treatment of Isaiah 7:14f by the book of Matthew, The Isaiah passage, written more than seven hundred years before

Christ, relates to the fast-approaching invasion of Israel by the Assyrians and predicts that before the event a young woman (*almah*) shall bear a son. It is important to observe that the Hebrew term *almah* signifies a young woman, either married or single, without any reference to her sexual experience. Consequently, the Jewish English Bible translates 'young woman.' When the Hebrew text itself mentions a virgin, *per se* it uses another form, *bethulah* . . .

"The Isaiah passage is used in the book of Matthew in the interests of Christian dogma, as a prediction of the birth of Jesus . . ." (*The Bible is Human*, pp. 11f).

According to the Gospels also Jesus' end is foretold in the Old Testament. Here the most rewarding text proved to be the fifty-third chapter of Isaiah, describing the tribulations of the "suffering servant" of the Lord who, as is evident from the text, is none other than Israel, afflicted so that she may serve and fulfill her mission the better. To Christianity, however, this chapter is the most compelling prediction of Jesus' sufferings and death. Especially such verses as, "He was despised and forsaken of men, a man of pains and acquainted with disease, as one from whom men hide their face; he was despised, and we esteemed him not. Surely our diseases he did bear, and our pain he carried; whereas we did esteem him stricken, smitten of God and afflicted. But he was wounded because of our transgressions, he was crushed because of our iniquities . . ." exerted an almost magic compulsion upon Christian minds, blinding them to the true meaning of this chapter.

Proof texts, however, were also adduced for minor incidents and episodes connected with the crucifixion. Thus Judas' betrayal of Jesus, his remorse, his turning over of the thirty silver pieces to the Temple, and the priests' purchase of the Potter's field as a burial ground with this money was regarded as fulfilment of some passages of the Prophet Zechariah

(11:12f) which the New Testament, however, wrongly ascribes to Jeremiah, probably because of the association of that earlier prophet's purchase of a field (see Matthew 27:9f).

The piercing of Jesus' side (John 19:37) is claimed to have been a fulfilment of Zechariah's prophecy "They have thrust him through" (12:10), referring in the text to Israel's defeat at the hands of the enemy; Professor Toy therefore admits: "The reference, by the evangelist, to the piercing of Jesus' side is based on a translation and exegesis of the Hebrew that cannot be maintained" (*Quotations in the New Testament*, p. 93).

According to the Gospels Jesus' legs were not broken, as was the Roman custom, when His body was taken off the cross. This, too, was proclaimed to be a fulfilment of a Scriptural passage, namely the prohibition of the breaking of the bones of the paschal lamb (Exodus 12:46; Numbers 9:12) and, more especially, of the Psalmist's solace to the righteous: "Many are the ills of the righteous, but the Lord delivereth him out of them all. He keepeth all his bones, not one of them is broken" (Psalms 34:20f). The New Testament utilizes this passage as follows: "But when they came to Jesus they saw that He was dead already, and they did not break His legs. . . . this happened to fulfill what the Scripture says: 'Not one of its bones will be broken'" (John 19:33–36). Thus Jesus' symbolic identification with the "paschal lamb" is based on the above quoted Hebrew Bible passages.

The Gospel according to John records: "When the soldiers had crucified Jesus, they took his clothes and divided them into four parts, one for each soldier, besides his shirt. Now his shirt had no seam; it was woven in one piece from top to bottom. So they said to one another, 'Let us not tear it, but let us draw for it, to see who gets it.' This was to fulfill what the Scripture says: 'They divided My garments among them, and for My clothing they cast lots'" (John 19:23f). The Scriptural quotation is from Psalm 22:19 where the righteous complains of the wrongs inflicted upon him by the wicked. Professor Toy has this to say on the New Testament use of that passage: "The Psalmist is surrounded by fierce enemies, who strip off his clothing, and share it among themselves. John, taking the psalm as messianic, regards this passage as a prediction of the division of the garments of Jesus among the soldiers who performed the crucifixion. The parallelism, however, is not a strict one; the soldiers took the garment, not out of enmity to him whom they crucified, but as customary perquisites. In Matthew 27:35, Mark 15:24, Luke 23:34, the dividing of the garments is mentioned, but there is no reference to the Old Testament (*Quotations in the New Testament,* pp. 90f).

The New Testament accounts which connect the crucifixion and its details with the Hebrew Bible are even more arbitrary than those attempting to adduce Hebrew Scriptural proofs for Jesus' career and ministry. This fact is rather frankly admitted by Professor Toy, who writes: "The height of arbitrary quotation is reached in the Epistle to the Hebrews, in which the free Alexandrian method of treating the Old Testament is visible. There are no bounds to the writer's ability to extract from his Greek version [of the Hebrew Bible] the sense which he desires; he goes so far as to find a demonstration of the necessity of the sacrifice of Christ (Hebrews 10:5–10) in a Psalm passage (Psalm 40:7) which affirms that God desires not sacrifice, but obedience to His will" (*Quotations in the New Testament,* pp. 138f).

The evidence adduced and passages considered should prove that the Bibles of Judaism and of Christianity are *not* the same. Those books which are sacred to both Christians and Jews, i.e., the Hebrew Bible, have an altogether different meaning for the former than for the latter. Even those Christians who do not accept all of the "arbitrary" (Toy's characterization) uses to which the Hebrew Bible text is put, still adhere to the thesis that the New Testament is the fulfillment of the Old Testament in a larger sense of greater human and religious perfection, a view to which Jews, of course, cannot assent. It is therefore illusory to speak of the Scriptures "shared" by Judaism and Christianity. The differences in the interpretation of the identical text really makes the Christian version of the Hebrew Bible an altogether different book.

CHAPTER VIII

Jesus

IN RECENT YEARS there have been sounded numerous direct and indirect appeals by Jewish literati, ranging from Sholem Asch, the erstwhile Yiddish novelist and now the most zealous propagator of Christian ideas, to John Cournos, the literary critic and convert to Christianity, to reclaim Jesus as a faithful son of the Jewish people and their religion. The argument advanced is that although Judaism may not be able to recognize the Christian claims of Messianic potency and Divine perfection for Jesus, still it could and should accept him as a prophet, a teacher, or as a great rabbi, at least.

Before proceeding to the detailed refutation of these suggestions, we must pause for a moment to consider Jesus' place in Christianity. Of course, the various Christian denominations differ in their interpretation of the founder of their faith. Yet even the most liberal Protestants, provided they have not left the ground of the Church, would hardly be ready to admit that Jesus was nothing else but a teacher, a prophet, or a rabbi. It is therefore mistaken on the part of certain Jews to assume that their endorsement of Jesus as a teacher, prophet, or rabbi will be instrumental in bringing about better relations between Christians and Jews. On the contrary most Christians deeply resent to have their Son of God and Messiah acclaimed as a mere mortal teacher, prophet, or rabbi. The attitude of the vast majority of Christians toward Jewish attempts to reclaim Jesus for the Synagogue is pithily summarized by Dr. Otto Piper: "The Jews may be willing to acknowledge the greatness of Christ, but they only seek thereby to emphasize the greatness of Judaism, for they vindicate Jesus as their greatest son. If they would recognize him as their Messiah and Savior, they would no longer be able to be Jews" (*God in History*, p. 106).

To Christians Jesus is infinitely more than a great prophet and teacher, for as Professor Toy aptly observed: "Both branches of Christianity, Catholic and Protestant, have followed the currents of modern thought; there is not a phase of science, philosophy, or literature but has left its impression on the body of the beliefs that control Christendom. But in all this freedom of movement the person of Christ has maintained its place as the center of religious life. Whatever the particular construction of the theology, whether he be regarded as substantially divine or only as a profoundly inspired man, whether his death or his life be most emphasized, whether Church or Bible be accepted as infallible guide, he is ever the leader and model of religious experience" (*Judaism and Christianity*, p. 435).

To Christians, save for an insignificantly small group of modernists, Jesus is, first of all, the Son of God and Messiah. He is to Christendom the revelation in the flesh of the perfection of God. To quote Dr. A. Lukyn Williams: "To us Christians, I repeat, Jesus of Nazareth appears to be absolutely faultless, without spot or blemish, and as such to be the one perfect revelation of the character of God. What God could not do in any book however good, He was able to do in a living person . . . When a Christian man is asked about the character of the invisible God, he points out in answer 'Jesus of Nazareth,' meaning that Jesus shows us what God really is like and loves us to do. The thought recalls Jesus' own saying reported in the Fourth Gospel—'He that hath seen me hath seen the Father'" (Williams, *The Modern Doctrines of Judaism Considered*, p. 55).

Christianity is predicated on the doctrine of the incarnation, that is to say, on the belief that "God was in Christ—not in writing or doctrines or miracles or subjective experiences or sacramental forms, but in a historic person, in Christ's spirit, his word, his life, his death" (Harris F. Rall, *Christianity*, p. 156). As a result, Christian virtue and perfection consist in "the imitation of Christ," whereas for the Jew goodness is bound up in the attempt to imitate by approximation the perfection of God, because Judaism knows of no incarnation of the Divine Being. Judaism therefore rejected, and rejects, Jesus as the Son of God and as an incarnation of the Divine Being. The Jewish God idea, as has been set forth in detail in the chapter "The Jewish and the Christian God Idea" (pp. 15ff), is the very negation of the Trinity and its underlying doctrine of incarnation.

But to Christians Jesus is not only the incarnation of God but also the Messiah and Redeemer whose future advent is announced in the books of the Hebrew Bible. The New Testament is therefore to a very large extent the concerted effort to prove that Jesus was the promised Messiah and that in him all the prophetic promises were fulfilled. Judaism on the other hand maintains that Jesus was not the Messiah for he did not fulfill the Messianic hopes. The defenders of Judaism in the "Religious Disputations," arranged by the medieval Church and forced upon the Jews in the hope of defeating their spokesmen, invariably stressed that not one of the Messianic promises was fulfilled through Jesus. He neither established universal peace and social justice for all of mankind nor did he redeem Israel and raise the Lord's mountain as the top of the mountains. As far as the Jews are concerned, their own exile and homelessness and the continuation of war, poverty and injustice are conclusive proof of the fact that the Messiah has not yet arrived, for his coming, according to the prophetic promises, will usher in the redemption of Israel from exile and the redemption of all the world from the evils of war, poverty and injustice.

It has been argued that Jesus did not regard himself as the Messiah and that this role was subsequently ascribed to him by the authors of the Gospels. We are not concerned here with New Testament criticism and it is beyond the scope of our theme to attempt to ascertain which utterances ascribed to Jesus are authentic, and which are not. What really matters are not the exact words that Jesus uttered but the spirit that informed them. There can be no doubt, however, that "in the Gospels we possess the *ipsissimus spiritus* of Jesus" (Prof. W. J. Lowstuter, *New Testament Studies*, edited by E. Prince Booth, 1942, p. 115). Ostensibly, the tradition connected with Jesus must have provided the authors of the Gospels with sufficient grounds to stress his messiahship—otherwise it would be inexplicable that all the Gospel accounts stress Jesus' own emphasis on his messianic role and mission. Jesus' answer to John the Baptist's query whether he was the one promised by the Prophets, clearly shows that Jesus did regard himself as the Messiah (Matthew 11:2–6). Also his reply to Simon Peter (Matthew 16:13–20) and, even more so, the admission at his trial before the High Priest to be "the Christ, the Son of God" (Matthew 26:63–66; Mark 14:61–64; Luke 22:67–71) conclusively prove that Jesus regarded himself as the Messiah, and, more than that, as the Son of God. These two pretensions placed him inevitably in eternal opposition to Judaism, which cannot recognize Jesus as the Messiah because of his failure to usher in the messianic era, and which rejects the very idea of a "Son of God" as an infringement upon pure monotheism.

CAN JESUS THEN QUALIFY, at least, as a "Prophet" from the Jewish point of view? The answer is negative for he did not live up to standards of Hebrew prophecy exemplified by the early and the later Prophets. The Hebrew Prophet was first and last the mouthpiece of God. None of the Prophets of Israel ever taught in his own name and on his own responsibility. The "I" of the Prophets is God; the "I" of Jesus, however, is he himself. He taught on his own authority, frequently in opposition to the authoritative teachings of the Rabbis of the time, and he stressed his own personal opinions beyond anything that had ever been heard in Israel. For no prophet or teacher ever prophesied or taught on his own authority. On the contrary, they endeavored to find justification for new teachings in the Torah. According to Jewish conviction, sounded by the Sages of the Talmud and authoritatively summarized by Maimonides, "a prophet must not 'add or diminish,' that is to say add or abrogate any of the Torah commandments." Jesus, however, did precisely that. His exaggerated overemphasis on ethics and his deliberate violation of the ritual law disqualified him as a prophet. For if the Prophets demanded justice rather than sacrifices as pleasing to God, they did not say that sacrifices are superfluous, but only stressed that God will not accept the offerings of the evil doers. Jesus, however, as we shall yet see, claimed the right to abrogate or change certain ritual laws and practices.

Jesus' emphasis on his own teachings, most of which are contrary to the very spirit of Hebrew prophecy, culminated in his claim to possess special nearness to God, a nearness not shared or even approximated by any other human being. Thus he declared: "Everything has been handed over to me by my Father, and no one understands the Son but the Father, nor does anyone understand the Father but the Son and anyone to whom the Son chooses to reveal him. Come to me, all of you who toil and are burdened, and I will let you rest. Let my yoke be put upon you, and learn from me, for I am gentle and humble minded, and your hearts will find rest, for the yoke I offer you is a kindly one, and the load I ask you to bear is light" (Matthew 11:27–30). No such words had ever been uttered by a Jewish prophet or teacher, for the claim contained in them is contrary to the Jewish democratic conviction that all men are equal before God, and that there is no particular "Son of God" who is nearer to the Father in Heaven than all the rest. The idea that one specific person should have the power to reveal, or not to reveal, as he "chooses" the understanding of God must have come as a shock to Jesus' Jewish contemporaries who were taught to regard God alone as the source of all truth.

The Gospels are studded with Jesus' claims to stand in a very special relation to God and with promises that those who believe in him will be rewarded by God. Thus we read:

"Everyone who will acknowledge me before men, I will acknowledge before my Father in heaven, but anyone who disowns me before men, I will disown before my Father in heaven" (Matthew 10:32f).

"If anyone is thirsty, let him come to me and drink. If anyone believes in me, streams of living water, as the Scripture says, shall flow forth from his heart" (John 7:37f).

"I have come into this world to judge men, that those who cannot see may see, and that those who can see may become blind" (John 9:39).

"I am the light of the world. Whoever follows me will not have to walk in darkness, but will have the light of life" (John 8:11f).

"As long as I am in the world, I am a light for the world" (John 9:5).

"I myself am Resurrection and Life. He who believes in me will live on, even if he dies, and no one who is alive and believes in me will ever die" (John 11:25f).

"I am Way and Truth and Life. No one can come to the Father except through me. If you knew me, you would know my Father also. From now on you do know Him and you have seen Him" (John 13:6f).

"Do you not believe that I am in union with the Father, and the Father is in union with me?" (John 13:10).

"Whoever hates me hates my Father also" (John 16:23).

There are many more utterances by Jesus coached in a similar vein. Ostensibly, they present an eternal and unbridgeable negation of the Jewish convictions and teachings which know of no special, privileged position of *any* person before God. God, as the Jew knows Him, is equally near to all men, His nearness depending upon how near they want Him to be to them, and how closely they wish to approach, by unrelenting ethical effort, His perfection. No Jewish prophet, not even Moses, "The Master of the Prophets," ever claimed to be nearer to God than any other man. The Prophets regarded themselves as servants of God, and they strove to discharge their call faithfully—but they kept their own personalities, their own loves and hates and ambitions, as much as it is possible for human beings to do so, apart from their mission. They were the mouthpieces of God, who had to proclaim His message, whether they wanted it or not, for the fire of the Divine inspiration was consuming their inwards. The call was so all-powerful that under its impact the personality of the Prophet was all but crushed and he became nothing but the chosen instrument of God—an instrument to be played upon by His Maker, but not to play on his own life's melody . . . .

THE DIFFERENCE between the Hebrew Prophets and Jesus is no less evident in their respective attitudes to sin and the sinners.

The traditional and perennial task of the Prophets was to castigate their contemporaries for their sins, but not to forgive sins. Jesus, however, arrogated to himself the power of forgiving sins, which Judaism reserves for God alone. Thus Jesus declared when healing a paralytic: "Which is easier to say, 'Your sins are forgiven,' or to say, 'Get up and walk'? But I would have you know that the Son of Man has the authority to forgive sins on earth" (Matthew 9:2–6). When Jesus told the woman of evil repute, "Your sins are forgiven," his table companions were shocked into asking: "Who is this man, who even forgives sins?" (Luke 7:48f), for such an intrusion upon a Divine prerogative was unheard of in Israel.

Jesus' accentuation of his own personality, the emphasis on "But *I* tell you. . .", rather than on the One by Whom he considered himself sent, led to it that at times he acted as if he himself were God, the master of sickness and health, of life and of death. Quite logically and inevitably the overemphasis of his own powers led Jesus to draw an analogy between himself and God, an analogy by means of which he claimed to command Divine powers: "For just as the Father awakens the dead and makes them come to life, the Son makes anyone whom He chooses come to life. For the Father passes judgment on no one, but has committed the judgment entirely to the Son, so that all men may honor the Son just as much as they honor the Father" (John 5:18–23). That these passages of the Fourth Gospel represent "the ipsissimus spiritus" of Jesus is amply attested by the records of some of his miraculous healings in the other Gospels. Thus, for instance, when the leper petitioned him, saying, "If you only choose, sir, you can cure me!" Jesus replied: "I do choose! Be cured!" (Matthew 8:1–3; Mark 1, 40; Luke 5, 12f). Here, as in his other miracle workings, Jesus represents himself as the one who performs the cure, revives the dead, or causes the miracles to come about.

The Hebrew Bible, too, knows of miracles performed by Prophets. But none of the Prophets ever wrought a miracle on his own authority, or represented it to be a sign of his own power and strength. The Hebrew Prophets invariably stressed that they were merely God's instruments in the performance of the miracle and that the credit for it was due not to them but to God. Thus when Pharaoh complimented Joseph on his ability to interpret dreams, Joseph replied: "It is not in me, God will give Pharaoh an answer of peace" (Genesis 41:16). All the miracles Moses performed he executed upon Divine command and when he once deviated from the Divine instruction and smote the rock instead of merely speaking to it, he was found guilty and severely punished. For, according to Jewish belief, man is merely the instrument of God in the performance of miracles and therefore he is not free to depart even an iota from the Divine command and instruction.

When Elijah caused the widow's jar of flour and her cruse of oil to last the entire length of the drought, he distinctly stressed that it was not he who caused that miracle. "For thus saith the Lord, the God of Israel: The jar of flour shall not be spent, neither shall the cruse of oil fail, until the day that the Lord sendeth rain upon the land" (I Kings 17:14). And when Elijah revived the son of the widow he did not convey the impression that he had wrought that miracle, as Jesus did on a similar occasion (see especially Matthew 9:23–26), but "he cried unto the Lord and said: 'O Lord my God, I pray Thee, let this child's soul come back to him.' And the Lord hearkened unto the voice of Elijah; and the soul of the child came back unto him, and he revived" (I Kings 17:21f). Similarly, we read in the story of Elisha that when he revived the son of the Shunamite, "he prayed unto God" and the child was revived in answer to his prayer (II Kings 4:33). God is thus enthroned as the reviver of the dead; the Prophet is merely his instrument.

The Gospels record that Jesus once turned five loaves of bread and two fish into food sufficient for five thousand men, and what was left over filled twelve baskets (Luke 9:13–17; compare John 6:10–13). In performing this miracle Jesus made no reference whatsoever to God, offering it as proof of his own powers. It is instructive to compare the story of Jesus' miraculous feeding of the multitudes with a similar account in the Hebrew Bible. Once Elisha was confronted with the necessity of feeding a hundred men with twenty loaves of barley and fresh ears of corn. When his servant despaired of managing under these trying conditions, Elisha told him: "Give the people that they may eat; for thus saith the Lord: 'They shall eat, and shall leave thereof.' So he set it before them, and they did eat, and left thereof, according to the word of God" (II Kings 4:42–44). Elisha credited God with this miracle, while Jesus, in an identical situation, performed it on his own authority, without any appeal to God and without assigining to Him the credit for it.

Jesus performed miracles to make the people believe in himself. The Hebrew Prophets wrought miracles to strengthen the belief in God.

When Moses wanted to cure Miriam of her leprosy, he "cried unto the Lord, saying: 'Heal her now, O God, I beseech Thee'" (Numbers 12:13). And when Elisha cured the Aramean General, Naaman, from leprosy, he made it so unmistakable that God had cured him that Naaman vowed "henceforth to offer neither burnt-offering nor sacrifice unto other gods, but unto the Lord" (II Kings 5:17). When performing miracles, the Prophets of Israel invariably made it understood that it was not they who produced the desired results but God, Who employed them as the tools of His will.

The Jewish contemporaries of Jesus, steeped in the tradition of their faith, therefore were repulsed rather than attracted and convinced by the miracles which he performed on his own authority.

The early Christian belief in Jesus was virtually wholly justified by the miracles he performed. In later centuries, too, Christianity has based its claims of possessing the truth on the wonders and signs performed by Jesus and the Apostles. And even today the Catholic Church still regards miracles as the acid test of the truth.

According to Jewish conviction, on the other hand, miracles do not prove a thing. Jewish teachers through the ages have emphasized that the truth cannot be established by magic and wizardry. To the Jew miracles are at best an *additional* affirmation of the truth, but he will refuse to accept them as the sole criterion of the correctness of a teaching or belief.

In the careers of the Hebrew Prophets miracles played an insignificant role. The Prophets resorted to miracles only in extremities, and then not to prove the truth but only to impress its validity upon certain types of people. It is characteristic of the Jewish estimate of the value of miracles that the Pentateuch relates that some of the plagues which Moses brought down on Egypt were also produced by Pharaoh's magicians, "who did the same with the secret arts" (Exodus 7:22). Thus the magicians turned water into blood, and they caused frogs to come up on the land of Egypt. Judaism therefore rejects the miracle as a conclusive test to establish the truth, for there is always the latent danger of magic and witchcraft lending a hand.

Then, also, Jesus' teachings did not measure up to the prophetic standards. Although he repeated many of the ethical maxims and lessons of the Prophets, his arbitrary dismissal of important points of Jewish law place him in the class of those "who add to or diminish from the Torah," a serious lapse from the traditional Jewish point of view.

Jesus' attitude to life and the laws by which it is to be regulated, according to the teachings of Judaism, differed greatly from that of the recognized Rabbis and authentic teachers of the Law of his day. The Gospels clearly show that Jesus felt himself in opposition to the Rabbis, "the Pharisees." Ostensibly, Jesus did not regard himself as a "Rabbi," nor was he interested in the fine points of the Law and its exposition which was the predominant interest of the Rabbis of the time.

Jesus' attitude to the principal social institutions and to the Law were such, however, that in themselves they sufficed to place him in eternal opposition to Judaism and its Rabbis. The Gospels furnish ample evidence that Jesus had little use and even less love for the Rabbis, for his views and attitudes were diametrically opposed to the Jewish philosophy and way of life.

JUDAISM IS ESSENTIALLY OPTIMISTIC. It teaches that life and the world are good and that piety consists in the spiritual and religious penetration of the physical and material rather than in total abnegation and asceticism.

Jesus was of an ascetic nature. His kingdom was not of this world and his teachings, therefore, were principally concerned with the world-to-come. While the Rabbis of his day endeavored to solve the problem of poverty by adequate social legislation and provision, Jesus, unconcerned with the problems presented by want, dealt with it merely from the unreal vantage point of the better world-to-come. To him poverty was not a deplorable and degrading condition calling for abolition, but, on the contrary, he regarded it as the passport, as it were, to the kingdom of heaven. And so he advised a would-be disciple: "If you want to be perfect, go!

Sell your property and give the money to the poor, and you will have riches in heaven. Then come back and be a follower of mine" (Matthew 19:21). Obviously, this is no solution of the problem of want and social suffering. On the contrary, it aggravates the problem by adding more paupers to the rank and file of those in want.

The social problem has agitated since the very earliest time the minds and the hearts of Jewish teachers. They attempted to solve it, and largely succeeded in that attempt, by enacting laws taxing the wealthy for the benefit of the poor. Besides and above taxation, however, the Jewish teachers also insistently stressed the importance of charity. Still they did not advocate that a man divest himself of all his possessions. On the contrary, they disparaged improvident open-handedness as unwise and contrary to the Law, laying down the rule that one should not give to charity more than one-fifth of his possessions.

The ideal human being of Judaism lives a full life as a member of his family, well integrated into the larger community, in the happy pursuit of a useful kind of work. In order to qualify as a follower of Jesus, however, one had to break with all ties of normal social life, for he demanded: "No one of you who does not say goodbye to all he has can be a disciple of mine" (Luke 14:33). This renunciation did not merely extend to material possession but also to the suppression of the most natural affections for the nearest members of the family.

In contradistinction to the positive Jewish attitude to marriage and the family, Jesus opposed them almost hostilely. He was unmarried and disparaged in extremely harsh words loyalty to parents, brothers and sisters, regarding such bonds as detracting from the love for God. The commandment to honor father and mother has invariably been upheld by the Rabbis and teachers as one of the most important laws of the

Torah. Jewish literature is replete with inspiring stories of the exemplary filial love and loyalty of the greatest Sages. Jesus, on the other hand, publicly disowned and shamed his mother and his brothers. Thus it is recorded that when he was addressing a crowd of people "his mother and his brothers came up and stood outside the crowd, wanting to speak to him. But he said to the man who told him, 'Who is my mother, and who are my brothers?' And he pointed to his disciples and said, 'Here are my mother and my brothers! For whoever does the will of my Father in heaven is my brother and my sister and my mother" (Matthew 12:46–50). On another occasion, when one of his listeners exclaimed, "Blessed be the mother who bore and nursed you!" Jesus replied, "You might better say, 'Blessed are those who hear God's message and observe it!'" (Luke 11:27f). He also taught: "You must not call anyone on earth your father, for you have only one father, your heavenly Father" (Matthew 23:9).

How Jesus applied these principles to actual life situations may be seen from his angry outbreaks against disciples who wanted to discharge certain filial and family obligations before following him. When a prospective disciple said to Jesus, "Master, I am going to follow you, but let me first say goodbye to my people at home," he reproved him, "No one who puts his hand to the plough, and then looks back, is fitted for the Kingdom of God" (Luke 9:61f).

In contradistinction to Judaism which expects the pious to take their places in society, as good sons, husbands, fathers, brothers and neighbors, Jesus demanded of his followers *to hate* their nearest and dearest in order to be better disciples. Accordingly he taught: "If anyone comes to me without hating his own father and mother and wife and children and brothers and sisters, and his very life too, he cannot be a disciple of mine" (Luke 14:26). To what extent Jesus wanted his disciples to go in disregarding all filial obligations may be judged from his answer to a disciple who requested: "Let me first go and bury my father." Jesus' reply was: "Follow me, and leave the dead to bury their own dead!" (Matthew 9:21f). Judaism makes the paying of the last respects to the dead an obligation of "lovingkindness." God Himself, in order to set an example for men, does not refrain from showing this lovingkindness to the dead. . . . Jesus' command to a disciple to let his father lie unburied until "the dead" (meaning those that did not accept Jesus' message) would bury him is contrary to the very spirit of Judaism.

Jesus' negative attitude to the most elementary duties children owe parents must be considered in the examination of the new kind of "love" he supposedly introduced. It is true, Jesus demanded, by going beyond the letter of Jewish law and without taking into consideration human nature, "love your enemies and pray for your persecutors" (Matthew 5:44). However, of what avail is this teaching if its promulgator also taught: "If anyone comes to me without hating his own father and mother . . . he cannot be a disciple of mine"? (Luke 14:26). Jewish law *does not* command that one love his adversary for this would be unnatural. It does, however, command to refrain from wreaking vengeance upon him and to assist him moreover in an emergency, for this is to be expected of a human being. Jewish law *does* insistently command love and respectful regard for parents, for husband and wife, for children, for brothers, sisters and all other members of one's family—and loving concern for all men.

"Christian love" is often placed in opposition to the "strict legalism" of Judaism. It is therefore in place to show that Jesus himself, as represented in the Gospels, more often than not failed to live up to the lofty principles which he preached. That Jesus was not above revenge, something that is forbidden by Jewish law, is evident from the fact that he threatened his opponents to disown them in the Kingdom of Heaven: "Then

I will say to them plainly, I never knew you! Go away from me, you who do wrong!" (Matthew 7:21–23). Judaism, the religion of "strict legalism," on the other hand represents God as drawing to Himself the repentant sinners without wanting to remember their former transgressions.

Jesus taught: "If anyone strikes you on your right cheek, turn him the other too; and if anyone wants to sue you for your shirt, let him have your coat too. And if anyone forces you to go one mile, go two miles with him" (Matthew 5:39–41). But he did not live up to this teaching. The Gospel also records his statement that he would requite good with good and evil with evil: "Everyone who will acknowledge me before men, I will acknowledge before my Father in heaven; but anyone who disowns me before men, I will disown before my Father in heaven" (Matthew 10:32f).

Another of his teachings to which Jesus himself failed to live up is the famous beatitude, "Blessed are the merciful, for they will be shown mercy" (Matthew 5:7). Jesus' and his disciples' attitude toward those who disagreed with them was anything but merciful, as is evident from their acrimonious hostility toward the Pharisees, to whom Jesus referred as "serpents" and "brood of snakes," threatening them moreover with eternal punishment in the hereafter (Matthew 23:19–33; and many similar passages). How far Jesus was from being merciful and free from revenge may be gauged from the fact that he even cursed a tree that did not yield the fruit he expected! Thus we read: "In the morning as he went back to the city, he grew hungry, and seeing a fig tree by the roadside, he went up to it, but found nothing on it but leaves. And he said to it, 'No more fruit shall grow on you!' and the fig tree withered up at once" (Matthew 21:18–20; Mark 11:13f).

That Jesus was far from the saintliness required for the readiness to repay good for evil is all too evident from his numerous parables and the direct threats to his enemies to see to their future punishment in the Kingdom of Heaven. Thus he envisioned himself as turning "in his splendor" to those who did not follow him on earth: "Begone, you accursed people, to the everlasting fire, destined for the devil and his angels! For when I was hungry, you gave me nothing to eat, and when I was thirsty you gave me nothing to drink, when I was a stranger, you did not invite me home, when I had no clothes, you did not supply me, when I was sick and in prison, you did not look after me" (Matthew 25:41–43).

There is also an irresolvable contradiction between Jesus' beatitude, "Blessed are the peace-makers, for they will be called God's sons" (Matthew 5:9) and his announcement: "Do not think that I have come to bring peace to the earth. I have not come to bring peace but a sword. For I have come to turn a man against his father and a daughter against her mother and a daughter-in-law against her mother-in-law, and a man's enemies will be in his own household" (Matthew 10:34–37; compare Luke 12:49–53).

THE HEBREW BIBLE regards all men as brothers through their common Father in Heaven. Accordingly the Prophets were God's messengers to all of mankind, and not merely to their own people. Jesus, on the other hand, introduced a definitely exclusive note by emphasizing that he was sent solely to "the lost sheep of the House of Israel" (Matthew 15:24). This particularism is even more pronounced in Jesus' refusal to heal the daughter of a Canaanite woman. The Hebrew Bible is replete with examples of deeds of kindness shown to non-Jews. To offer but one: When Naaman, the Aramean general who was stricken with leprosy, turned for help to the King of Israel, the Prophet Elisha rightaway offered his services and restored him to health, thanks to Divine grace (II Kings 5). The fact that Naaman was not an Israelite did not keep the

Prophet from helping him. Similarly, all Jewish codes of law and ethical guides stress that Jews must not discriminate against non-Jews, but give them assistance in adversity, sickness and tragedy, even as they would help Jews.

Jesus' harsh reply to the Canaanite woman was contrary to the accepted Jewish tradition no less than to the applied standards of Jewish ethics. For when the woman pleaded: "Take pity on me, sir! My daughter is dreadfully possessed by a demon!" Jesus did not comfort her but bade his disciples, "Send her away, for she keeps screaming after us," adding "I am sent only to the lost sheep of the House of Israel." When the stricken mother kept on pleading, he spoke the cruel words: "It is not right to take the children's bread and throw it to the dogs!" implying that non-Jews are dogs and consequently not entitled to Divine mercy. Only when the poor woman humbled herself to the extent of accepting the role of a dog, saying: "Even the dogs eat the scraps that fall from their masters' table," did Jesus relent and he promised to help her "because you have great faith" (Matthew 15:22–28; compare Mark 7:25–28). But even when he did help her he did so not out of humaneness and pity, but to repay that woman for her great faith in him personally.

Just as his inconsistencies and his opposition to certain essentials of Jewish belief and ethics placed Jesus in opposition to Judaism, so his arbitrary interpretations of certain all-important laws would disqualify him as a "rabbi" or "teacher." We have seen that Jesus' avowal that he had not come to do away with the Law or the Prophets was nullified by the parables of the new patch that cannot be affixed to an old garment and of the new wine that cannot be stored in old barrels.

Although Jesus pledged that not one dotting on an *i* or crossing of a *t* should be dropped from the Law, he himself disregarded and violated a number of important laws. We have already considered the illegality of authorizing his disciples to pick the heads of wheat on the Sabbath, for being hungry is not an emergency that would warrant the breaking of the Sabbath rest. We have also seen that in the enumeration of the ten commandments, Jesus omitted the four commandments of ceremonial duties. This, however, was only part of Jesus' deliberate disregard of the Law.

On a number of occasions he cured persons *not dangerously ill* on the Sabbath, claiming to be entitled to do so in opposition to the Rabbis who maintained that the Sabbath may (must, in fact!) be violated only for the sake of saving and preserving life, but not to treat chronically ill persons who have been in such a state for years and who, without any danger to life and health, can wait a few more hours, until the Sabbath is over. (See Matthew 12:9–14; Luke 13:10–16; Luke 14:3–6).

Jewish law sanctions and recommends divorce as a means of terminating an unhappy and untenable marriage. In point of fact, Jewish law is remarkably liberal for it accepts as a ground for divorce, the only cause of the failure of marriages and which is yet not admitted by the statutes of ever so many progressive states as a ground for divorce, namely incompatibility. The underlying motive is, of course, that it is cruel and immoral to force two persons who no longer love and respect each other to dwell under the same roof. The extremely fine sensibility of the Jew for the sacredness of the marriage bond may be seen from the fact that Jewish law prohibits marital intimacies if the husband hates his wife "in his heart." Divorce is a tragedy, this all Jewish teachers readily admitted. It is so tragic, in fact, that the very altar of God sheds tears when a man divorces the wife of his youth. But life being what it is, divorce is necessary nevertheless. And so Jewish law sanctions it and the Talmud devotes an entire tractate to the important legal implications of the dissolution of marriage (*Gittin*).

Jesus, in clear opposition to biblical and talmudic law,

prohibited divorce, except in case of adultery, on his own authority. Thus he taught: "They [the Jews] were told, 'Anyone who divorces his wife must give her a certificate of divorce.' But I tell you that anyone who divorces his wife on any ground except unfaithfulness, makes her commit adultery, and anyone who marries her after she is divorced commits adultery" (Matthew 5:31f; compare Matthew 19:3–9). As is well known, Catholicism still adheres to the letter of this principle and does not permit divorce.

Even more serious, however, was Jesus' negative attitude to the dietary laws expressed in his teaching: "Listen to this and grasp it! It is not what goes into a man's mouth that pollutes him; it is what comes out of his mouth that pollutes a man!" (Matthew 15:11). Obviously, this amounted to a clear and unequivocal disavowal of the dietary laws as unimportant. Jesus' disciples, stunned by this attack on one of the most important of Jewish observances, queried their master:

"Do you know that the Pharisees were shocked to hear you say that?" To which he replied: "Any plant that my heavenly Father did not plant must be uprooted! Leave them alone. They are blind guides! But if one blind man leads another, they will both fall into the ditch."

Upon Peter's request to explain the parable, Jesus said: "Have even you no understanding yet? Can you not see that whatsoever goes into the mouth passes into the stomach and then is disposed of? But the things that come out of the mouth come from the heart, and they pollute a man" (Matthew 15:12–18). Quite naturally, therefore, Jesus declared "all food clean" (Mark 7:19). Obviously, this frontal attack upon the whole body of the dietary laws forms a strange contrast with Jesus' avowal that he had not come to abolish anything of the Law or the Prophets. . . . By conveying the impression that the keeping of the dietary laws is irrelevant as against the faithful observance of the ethical laws, Jesus placed himself in eternal opposition to Judaism which teaches that the ceremonial law is the helpmeet of the ethical law, as it were, and its guardian.

Jesus also declared the ritual washing of hands before meals as unimportant. This is evident from his controversy with the Pharisees on this point of observance:

"Then some Pharisees and scribes came to Jesus from Jerusalem, and said to him, "Why do your disciples break the rules handed down by our ancestors? They eat bread without first washing their hands" (Matthew 15:1–3; compare Mark 7:1ff). In reply Jesus showered abuse upon the Pharisees, accusing them of neglecting the important ethical commandments for the sake of mere ritual regulations, although "it is these things that pollute a man, but not eating with unwashed hands" (Matthew 15:12).

However, not only Jesus' disciples but also he himself ignored the commandment of the washing of the hands. Once, as a guest at the house of a Pharisee, he sat down to the meal without washing his hands. When his host expressed his amazement at such an action, Jesus again levelled a bitter attack against the Pharisees: "You Pharisees clean the outside of cups and dishes, but inside you are full of greed and sickness. You fools! Did not the Creator of the outside make the inside too?" (Luke 11:37–41).

Jesus also placed himself in opposition to the Law and its teachers by ignoring fasts observed by the community and by advocating a departure from the customs connected with Jewish fasts. The Gospels record that when the Pharisees and even John the Baptist's disciples were fasting, Jesus' disciples did not fast. Upon being called to account for this laxity, Jesus replied that as long as he, "the bridegroom" dwelled with his disciples there was no reason why they should fast. For "can the sons of the bridal-chamber fast, while the bridegroom is with them? As long as they have the bridegroom with them they cannot fast. But the days will come when the bridegroom shall be taken away from them, and then will they fast in that day" (Matthew 9:14f; Mark 2:18–20; Luke 5:33–35).

The laws regulating the observance of Jewish fasts prohibit washing and perfuming as physical delights that should be shunned on days of solemn abnegation. Jesus, however, told his disciples to disregard these laws. "When you fast, do not put on a gloomy look, like the hypocrites, for they neglect their personal appearance to let people see that they are fasting. I tell you, that is all the reward they will get. But when you fast, perfume your hair and wash your face, so that no one may see that you are fasting, except your Father. . . ." (Matthew 6:16–18).

Judaism regards the community prayer as the most desirable form of worship. The *Minyan*, the prayer community of at least ten adult males, is the quorum required for certain important prayers and, especially, for the reading of the Torah on the prescribed days of every week. The emphasis placed on the prayer community of the *Minyan* does not imply, however, that Judaism is unaware or disdainful of the religious value and of the comfort to be derived from silent devotion. The importance attached to the *Minyan* is due to the fact that Judaism wants its confessors to know and realize always and ever that the individual is but a link in the mighty chain of his people and of humanity—and so should draw near to God, not alone and in solitude, but together with his brethren whose destiny is bound to his.

Jesus, in opposition to hallowed tradition, decried the religious value of the community prayer and idealized solitary devotion. "When you pray, you must not be like the hypocrites, for they like to pray standing in the synagogues and in the corners of the square, to let the people see them. I tell you, that is the only reward they will get! But when you pray, go into your own room and shut the door, and pray to your Father who is unseen, and your Father who sees what is secret will reward you" (Matthew 6:5f).

These examples of Jesus' hostile opposition to and non-conformance with basic Jewish laws and accepted principles, customs and ceremonies should prove conclusively that the title of "Rabbi" cannot be applied to him. Jesus, in fact, was opposed to and attacked all and everything the Rabbis of his time stood for. He opposed them not only in regard to some minor details and aspects of the Law but on principle and unqualifiedly. Thus Jesus warned his disciples against "the yeast of the Pharisees and Sadducees." And his followers understood correctly "that he was warning them not against yeast but against the teaching of the Pharisees and Sadducees" (Matthew 16:11f).

Our examination of Jesus' attitude to Judaism, its Law and its way of life has shown that he can qualify neither as a prophet, nor as a rabbi and teacher in the Jewish sense. In all important respects Jesus placed himself in opposition to the faith into which he was born. It is therefore idle and futile to make room for him in Judaism which he himself rejected in theory and practice, even though at times he insisted on being faithful to the religion of his fathers, a claim that is irrefutably controverted by the testimony of the Gospels.

Index

A

B

M

Mackay, John, on Jesus as God, 21

Magic, miracles as, 127

Maimonides

on asceticism, 63

on deliberate impoverish-
ment, 67–68

on eternal validity of Torah, 90

on ethical freedom, 41–42

on incorporeality of God, 19, 20

on joy in Law, 86

on miracles, 29, 31, 34

on moderation, 64

on Moses as human, 26, 27

on prophet's role, 121

on unknowability of God, 18–19

on well-being of body and soul,
86

Manasseh, as penitent, 60–61

Manna, 30

Marlatt, Earl B., Judaism interpreted by, 97–98

Marriage

Christian vs Jewish attitudes
toward, 65–67

divorce and, 135–136

hostility of Jesus to, 66, 129

Mary

attitude of Jesus to, 129–130

as mediator, 53

"Virgin Birth," and, 35,
112–113

worship of, 24, 27–28

Mediator role

in Catholicism vs. Protestantism,
53

of Jesus, 52, 53, 59, 107

Jewish view of, 53–55, 57

Melanchthon, Luther's letter to, 58

Men, separation of women from,
74

Mendelssohn, Moses, on miracles,
35

Mercy

as attribute of God, 59

Lazarus parable and, 70

revenge vs., 131–133

Messiah

Biblical "predictions" of, 101,
107–115

false, poverty and, 67

Jesus as, 99, 102, 110, 119–121

punishment of Jews for rejection
of, 99, 107

as still to come, 119–120

Messianic Age, miracles and,
34–35

Messianism, faith and, 8

Micah, Bethlehem prophecy, 110

Minyan, importance of, 138

Miracles, 29–38

allegorical view of, 30–31

cults based on, 36

distrust of, 34–35, 127

faith and belief in, 35–36

importance of in Christianity,
35–38, 127

importance of ethical teachings
vs., 32

Jesus and, 35, 124–127

by Pharaoh's magicians, 127

as prophetic visions, 31–32

Prophets and, 125–127

rationalization of, 29–32

religious value of, 32–33

sacraments and, 36–37

reason vs. belief as path to,
35–36

U

Uniqueness of God. *See* Unity
of God
Unity of God, 15–16
divisibility vs., 21–22
incarnation vs., 21–22, 23
as only known, 17
Universality of God, 22
Prophets and, 133
Unknowability of God, 16–19

V

Vengeance, 69–71, 131–133
"Vicarious atonement," 50–51,
56
ethical regeneration vs., 60
personal responsibility vs., 51–52
rejection of Law by, 79, 80
"Virgin Birth," 35, 112–113
Virginity, "innocence" equated
with, 65
Virtue, belief as required for,
48–49
Von Harnack, Adolph, on
"chosenness," 94–95
Vow of poverty, 68

W

Wallis, Louis D., on Isaiah passage,
112
War, arrival of Messiah and, 120
Washing of hands, denial of
importance of, 137
Water-drawing festival, 73–74
Wealth, piety and, 67, 68, 69–71
Williams, A. Lukyn
on atonement, 55–56
on Jesus, 118–119
Wine, sacramental, belief in
miracles and, 36
"Wisdom of Sirach," on ethical
freedom, 39–40
Witness requirement, Jesus and,
106–107
Women, separation of men from, 74
Worldliness, piety and, 68–69,
71–72
World-to-come, reliance on vs.
social action, 128–129

Z

Zechariah
Messiah prophecy, 111
piercing prophecy, 114
potter's field and, 113–114